ESSENTIAL ELEMENTS for Band

COMPREHENSIVE BAND METHOD

TIM LAUTZENHEISER • JOHN HIGGINS • CHARLES MENGHINI
PAUL LAVENDER • TOM C. RHODES • DON BIERSCHENK

Band is...

M aking music with a family of lifelong friends.
U nderstanding how commitment and dedication lead to success.
S haring the joy and rewards of working together.
I ndividuals who develop self-confidence.
C reativity—expressing yourself in a universal language.

Band is...**MUSIC!**

Strike up the band,
Tim Lautzenheiser

HISTORY OF THE ELECTRIC BASS

The invention of the Electric Bass (1950) is credited to one man, Leo Fender, a California guitar maker who wanted to create an amplified version of the double (string) bass. In its early years, the Electric Bass, also known as the Fender Bass or Bass Guitar, was used primarily for popular dance bands and early rock 'n roll groups.

Today, the Electric Bass has become one of the most popular instruments and is found in many types of music groups - jazz and rock bands, pit orchestras, sacred music, and even marching bands. Its distinct, amplified sound is considered to be one of the most significant influences on musical style in the last 40 years.

Most Electric Basses have four strings, tuned to the same pitches as a double bass. Recently, five and six string basses have become common with players who want to expand the range and versatility of the instrument.

Many players have become well known because of their innovative, distinctive bass lines with the Electric Bass: Paul McCartney (The Beatles), James Jamerson (Motown), Jaco Pastorius (Jazz/Fusion), Victor Wooten (Contemporary/Funk), Marcus Miller (Funk/R&B), Geddy Lee (Progressive Rock), Hadrian Feraud (Jazz/Fusion) and Thundercat (Various).

ISBN 979-835012071-4

THE BASICS

Posture

Sit on the edge of your chair, and always keep your:

- Spine straight and tall
- Shoulders back and relaxed
- Feet flat on the floor

Instrument & Left Hand Position

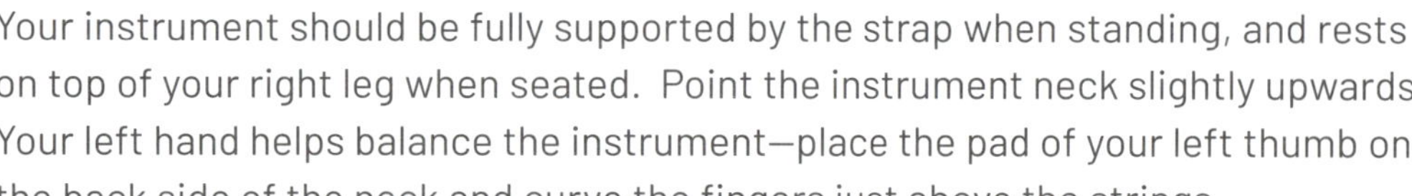

Your instrument should be fully supported by the strap when standing, and rests on top of your right leg when seated. Point the instrument neck slightly upwards. Your left hand helps balance the instrument—place the pad of your left thumb on the back side of the neck and curve the fingers just above the strings.

Producing The Essential Tone

Good bass players learn to produce a clean sound with a clear start to each tone and an even volume between tones. Except for the 4 open strings, your left hand "selects" a note by pressing down a string just behind a fret, and holding it for the entire length of the note. Your right hand "plays" the note by pulling across the string to start it vibrating.

STARTING THE TONE

- Rest your thumb on the E (largest) string or on the top edge of the pickup.
- Pull across the G (smallest) string with your index finger so that the finger comes to rest on the next string (D).
- Make the same tone by playing the G string with your middle finger.
- Play 2 tones on each string, with alternating index finger/middle finger.
- Strive for an even volume and clear start to each tone.

STOPPING THE TONE (DAMPENING)

- Stop a tone by gently touching the string with either hand.
- Fretted tones can also be stopped by lifting the left hand finger which was pressing down the string, but keeping the finger on the string.

Taking Care Of Your Instrument

- Be sure your amplifier is turned off before plugging-in or unplugging the audio cable connecting it to your instrument.
- When unplugging a cable, hold it by the plug (not by the wire).
- After playing, wipe off the instrument and strings with a clean soft cloth. Return the instrument to its case.
- Close all the latches on your case when the instrument is inside.
- Keep all 4 strings in tune (at normal tension) to prevent warping of the neck.
- Your case is designed to hold only specific objects. If you force anything else into the case, it may damage your instrument.

TUNING THE ELECTRIC BASS

Tuning means setting the correct pitch (higher or lower tone) of each string. This is adjusted by tightening or loosening the tuning keys on the head of the bass. Your teacher can help you tune to the 4 notes on the online audio, or to the notes on a piano:

Note:	E	A	D	G
String:	4	3	2	1 (highest)

Many bass players use an **Electronic Tuner** which "listens" to each string and indicates whether it is too high or low. You can learn to use **Relative Tuning** by comparing one string with another. After one string is tuned, it is compared with the pitch of the next lower string played with the 5th fret. The two pitches should match exactly.

See inside front cover for information on accessing instructional videos.

Getting It Together

Step 1 Securely attach the strap to the strap buttons, adjusting it so that the bass is at the correct height (approximately waist-high) and playing angle.

Step 2 With the amplifier off, plug the audio cable into the bass and the amplifier. Turn on the amplifier and set the volume.

Step 3 LEFT HAND: Place the pad of your left thumb on the back side of the neck. Your fingers should be relaxed and curved, just above the strings.

Step 4 RIGHT HAND: Rest your right thumb on the E (largest) string or on the top edge of the pickup. Rest the pad of your index finger on the G (smallest) string.

Step 5 Always sit or stand tall when playing, with feet flat on the floor and with arms and shoulders relaxed. Check your playing position with the illustrations:

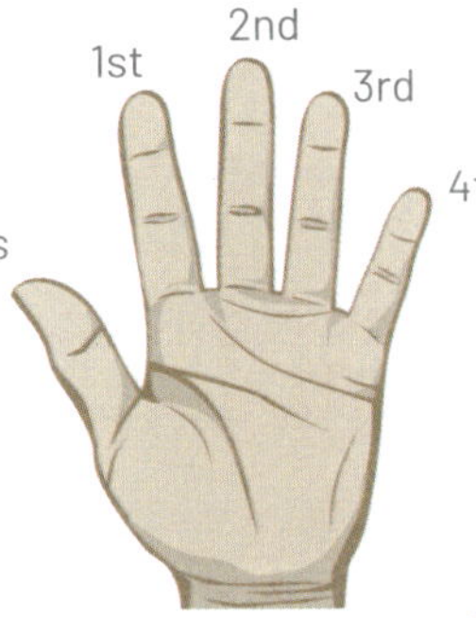

1st 2nd 3rd 4th

Think of your fingers as being numbered 1 through 4.

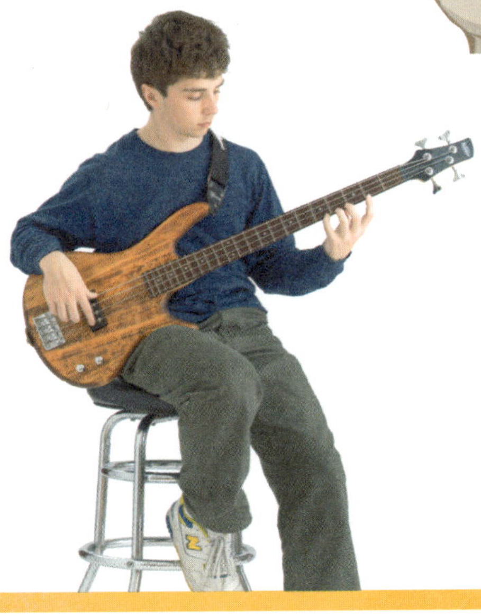

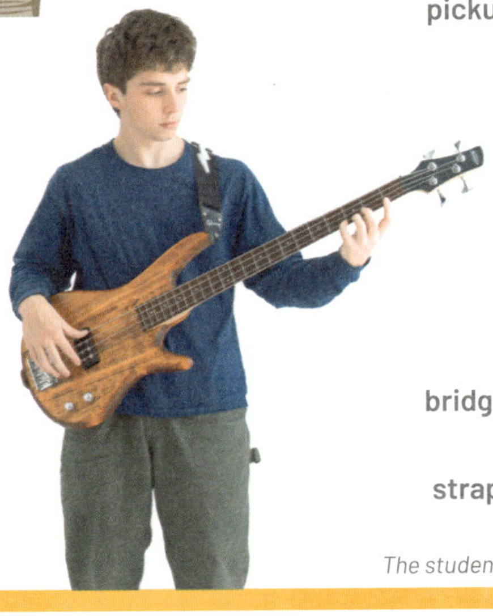

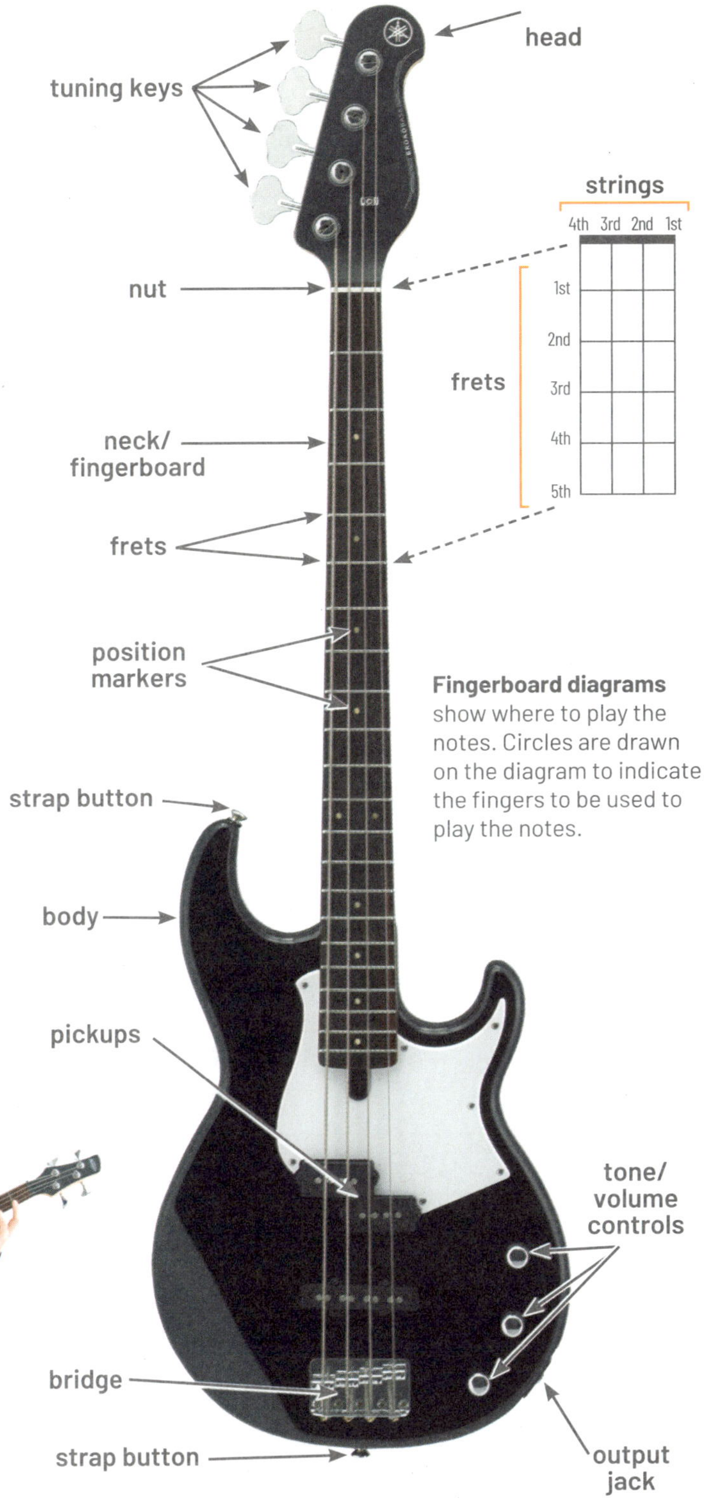

head

tuning keys

nut

neck/ fingerboard

frets

position markers

strap button

body

pickups

bridge

strap button

tone/ volume controls

output jack

strings

4th 3rd 2nd 1st

frets

1st 2nd 3rd 4th 5th

Fingerboard diagrams show where to play the notes. Circles are drawn on the diagram to indicate the fingers to be used to play the notes.

The student shown is a member of the Milwaukee Youth Symphony Orchestra.

READING MUSIC

Identify and draw each of these symbols:

Music Staff

The **music staff** has 5 lines and 4 spaces where notes and rests are written.

Ledger Lines

Ledger lines extend the music staff. Notes on ledger lines can be above or below the staff.

Measures & Bar Lines

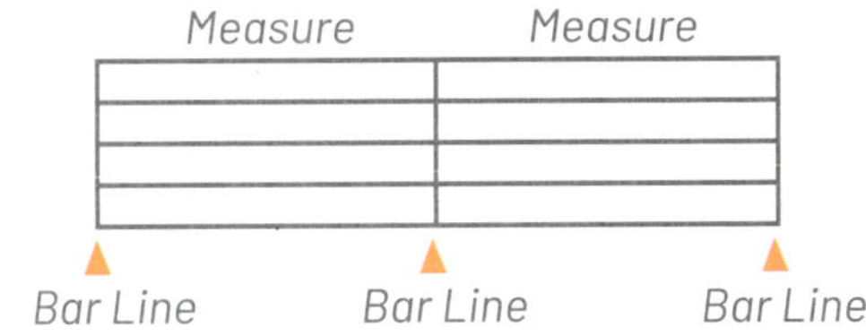

Bar lines divide the music staff into **measures**.

Long Tone

To begin, we'll use a special "Long Tone" note. Hold the tone until your teacher tells you to rest. Practice long tones each day to develop your sound.

1. THE FIRST NOTE

Hold each long tone until your teacher tells you to rest.

F — REST — F — REST

▲ *To play "F," place your fingers on the string as shown.*

The Beat

The **beat** is the pulse of music, and like your heartbeat it should remain very steady. Counting aloud and foot-tapping help us maintain a steady beat. Tap your foot **down** on each number and **up** on each "&."

One beat = 1 &
↓ ↑

Notes & Rests

Notes tell us how high or low to play by their placement on a line or space of the music staff, and how long to play by their shape. **Rests** tell us to count silent beats.

Quarter Note = 1 beat

Quarter Rest = 1 silent beat

2. COUNT AND PLAY

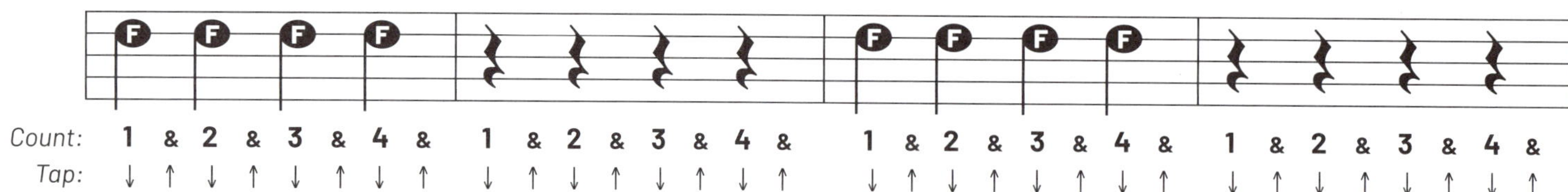

Count: 1 & 2 & 3 & 4 & | 1 & 2 & 3 & 4 & | 1 & 2 & 3 & 4 & | 1 & 2 & 3 & 4 &
Tap: ↓ ↑ ↓ ↑ ↓ ↑ ↓ ↑ | ↓ ↑ ↓ ↑ ↓ ↑ ↓ ↑ | ↓ ↑ ↓ ↑ ↓ ↑ ↓ ↑ | ↓ ↑ ↓ ↑ ↓ ↑ ↓ ↑

3. A NEW NOTE

Look for the fingering diagram with each new note. This note is "E♭ (E-flat)."

4. TWO'S A TEAM

Count & Tap: 1 & 2 & 3 & 4 & | 1 & 2 & 3 & 4 & | 1 & 2 & 3 & 4 & | 1 & 2 & 3 & 4 &

5. HEADING DOWN

Practice long tones on each new note.

D

6. MOVING ON UP

Count & Tap: 1 & 2 & 3 & 4 & | 1 & 2 & 3 & 4 & | 1 & 2 & 3 & 4 & | 1 & 2 & 3 & 4 &

Double Bar indicates the end of a piece of music.

Repeat Sign 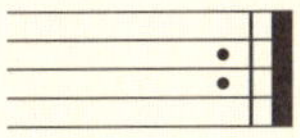 Without stopping, play once again from the beginning.

7. THE LONG HAUL

C

Double Bar

C REST C REST

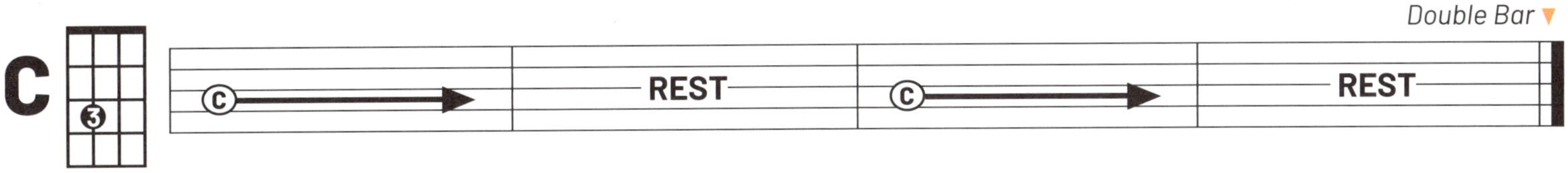

8. FOUR BY FOUR

Repeat Sign

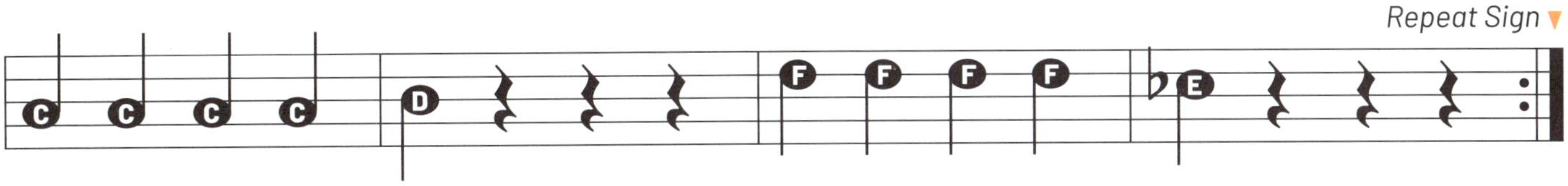

C C C C | D | F F F F | ♭E

Count & Tap: 1 & 2 & 3 & 4 & 1 & 2 & 3 & 4 & 1 & 2 & 3 & 4 & 1 & 2 & 3 & 4 &

9. TOUCHDOWN

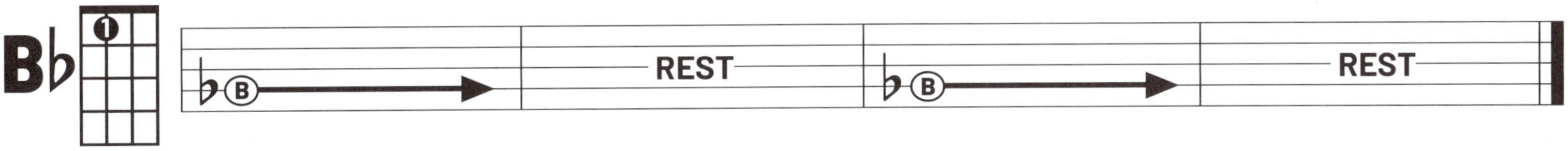

B♭

♭B REST ♭B REST

10. THE FAB FIVE

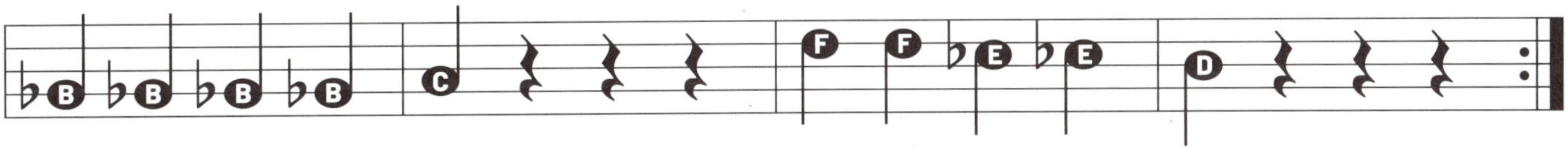

♭B ♭B ♭B ♭B | C | F F ♭E ♭E | D

1 & 2 & 3 & 4 & 1 & 2 & 3 & 4 & 1 & 2 & 3 & 4 & 1 & 2 & 3 & 4 &

Bass Clef (F Clef) indicates the position of note names on a music staff: Fourth line is F.

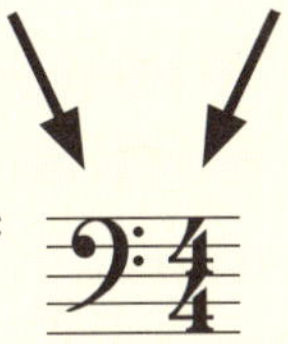

Time Signature indicates how many beats per measure and what kind of note gets one beat.

= **4 beats** per measure
= **Quarter** note gets one beat

Note Names Each note is on a line or a space of the staff. These note names are indicated by the Bass Clef.

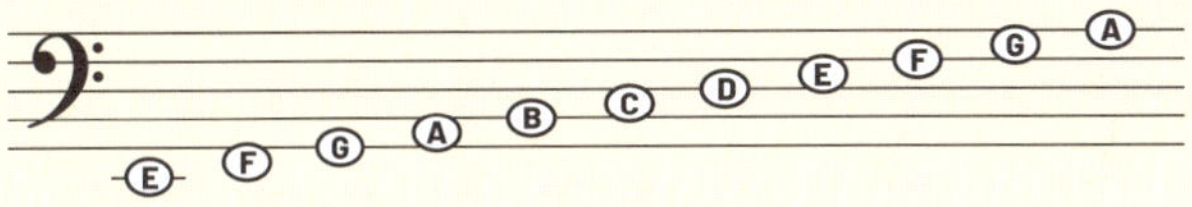

E F G A B C D E F G A

Sharp ♯ raises the note and remains in effect for the entire measure.

Flat ♭ lowers the note and remains in effect for the entire measure.

Natural ♮ cancels a flat (♭) or sharp (♯) and remains in effect for the entire measure.

THEORY

11. READING THE NOTES *Compare this to exercise 10, THE FAB FIVE.*

1 & 2 & 3 & 4 & 1 & 2 & 3 & 4 & 1 & 2 & 3 & 4 & 1 & 2 & 3 & 4 &

12. FIRST FLIGHT

13. ESSENTIAL ELEMENTS QUIZ *Fill in the remaining note names before playing.*

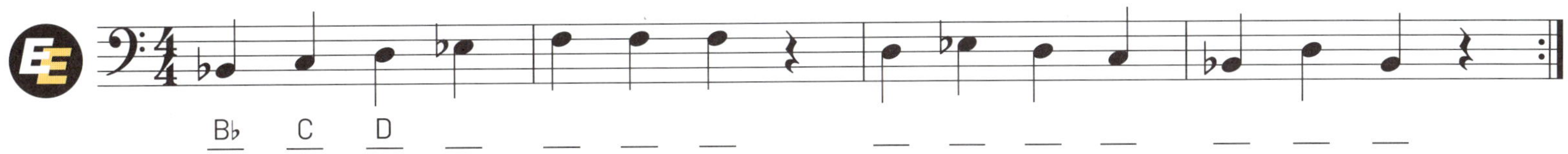

Notes In Review

Memorize the fingerings for the notes you've learned:

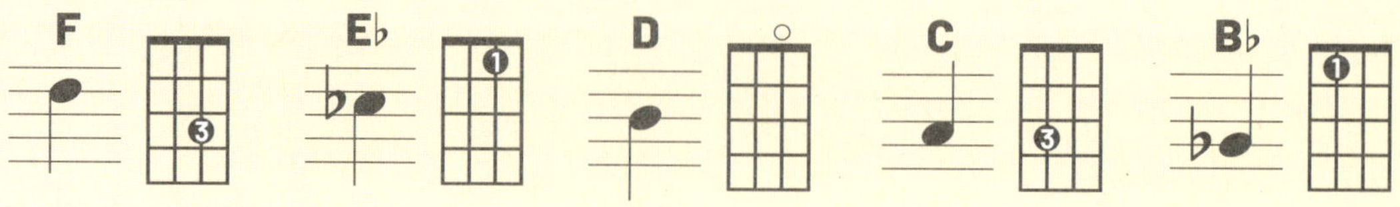

F · E♭ · D · C · B♭

14. ROLLING ALONG

Strive for a consistent sound with each note.

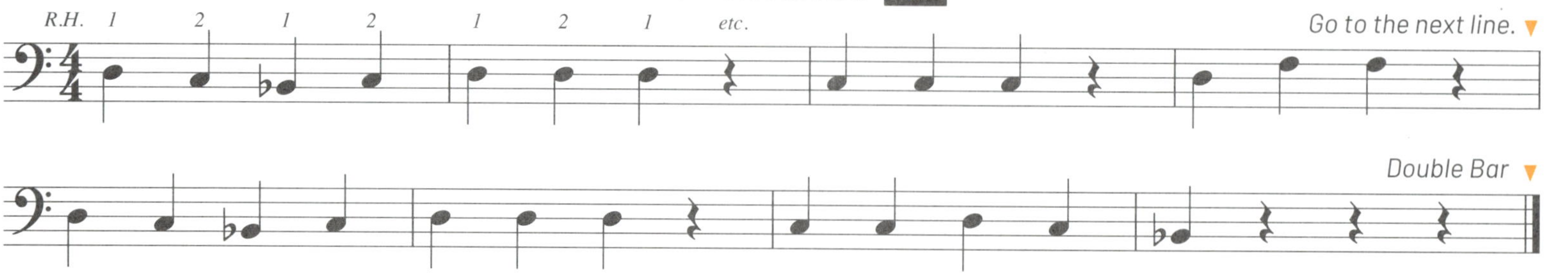

R.H. 1 2 1 2 1 2 1 etc.

Go to the next line. ▼

Double Bar ▼

Half Note

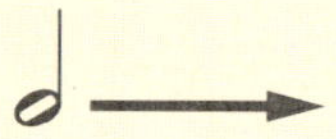

= 2 Beats

1 & 2 &

Half Rest

= 2 Silent Beats

1 & 2 &

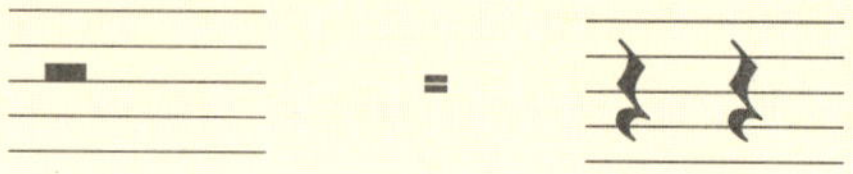

=

15. RHYTHM RAP

Clap the rhythm while counting and tapping.

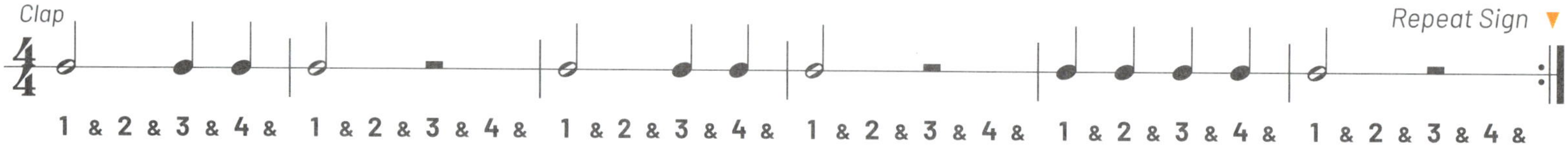

Clap

Repeat Sign ▼

1 & 2 & 3 & 4 & 1 & 2 & 3 & 4 & 1 & 2 & 3 & 4 & 1 & 2 & 3 & 4 & 1 & 2 & 3 & 4 & 1 & 2 & 3 & 4 &

16. THE HALF COUNTS

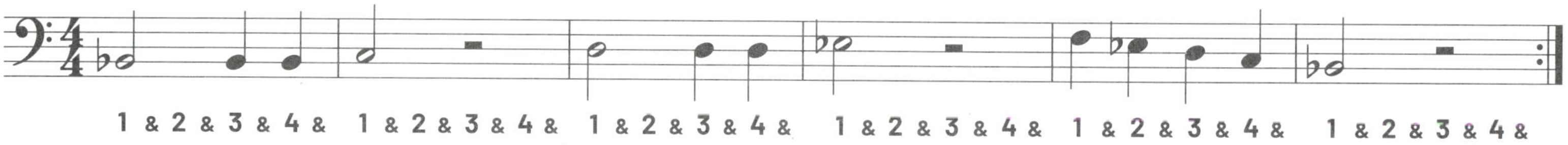

1 & 2 & 3 & 4 & 1 & 2 & 3 & 4 & 1 & 2 & 3 & 4 & 1 & 2 & 3 & 4 & 1 & 2 & 3 & 4 & 1 & 2 & 3 & 4 &

17. HOT CROSS BUNS

18. GO TELL AUNT RHODIE

Try this right hand technique, repeating fingers and alternating fingers. American Folk Song

19. ESSENTIAL ELEMENTS QUIZ

Using the note names and rhythms below, draw your notes on the staff before playing.

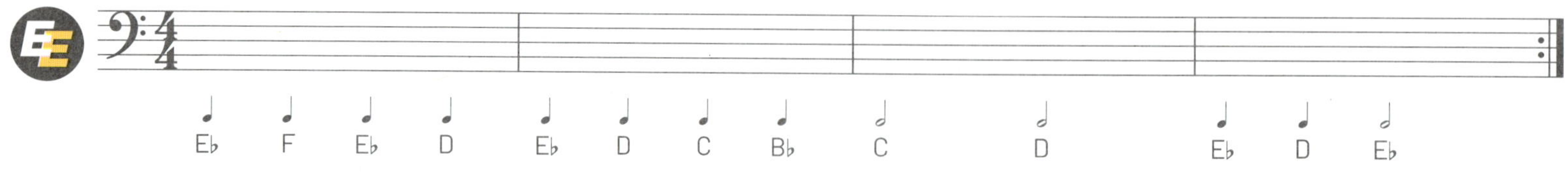

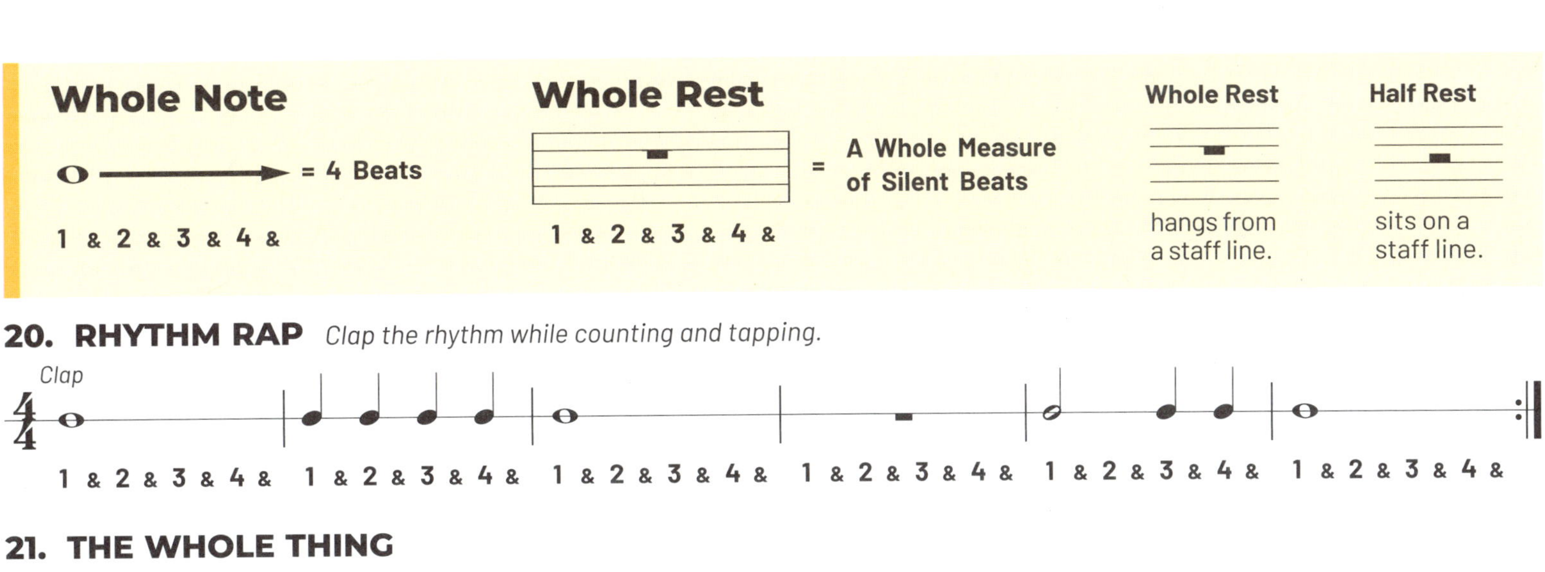

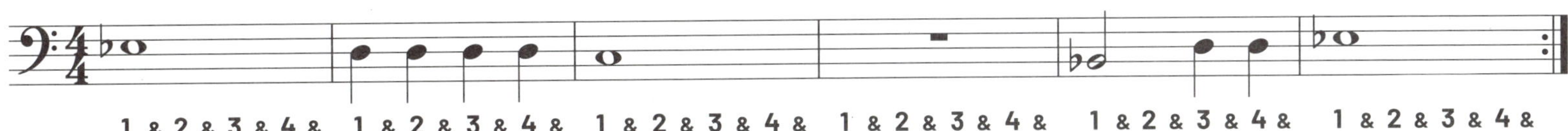

Duet A composition with two different parts, played together.

22. SPLIT DECISION – Duet

Key Signature

The **Key Signature** tells us which notes to play with sharps (♯) or flats (♭) throughout the music. Your Key Signature indicates the *Key of B♭* – play all B's as B-flats, and E's as E-flats.

THEORY

23. MARCH STEPS

R.H. 1 2 1 2 1 1 2 1 2 1 etc.

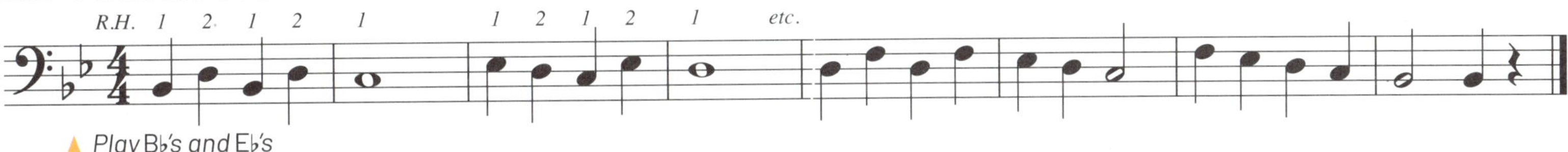

Play B♭'s and E♭'s

24. LISTEN TO OUR SECTIONS

Percussion Woodwinds Brass Percussion Woodwinds Brass Perc. Ww. Brass All

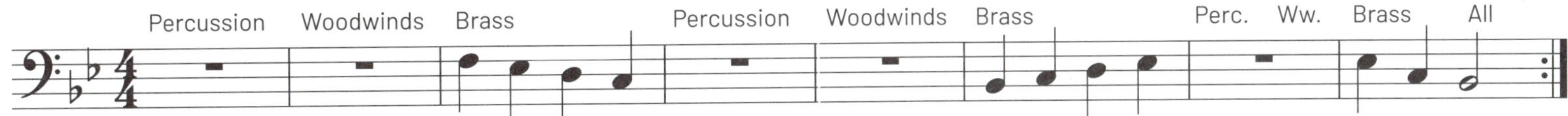

25. LIGHTLY ROW

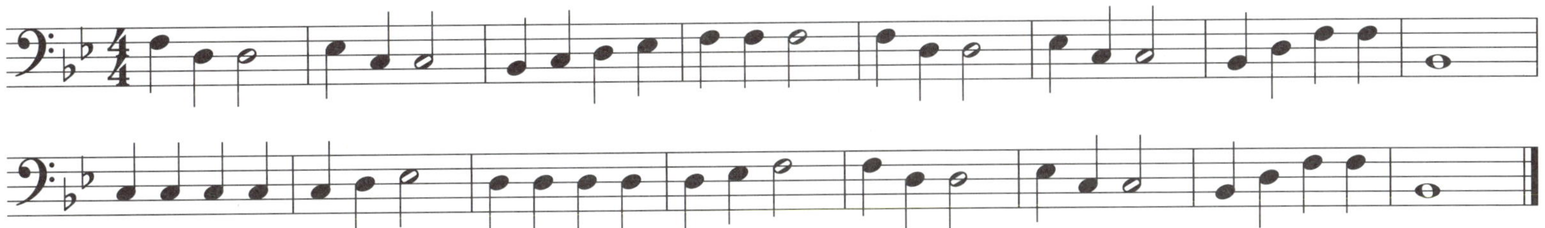

26. ESSENTIAL ELEMENTS QUIZ *Draw in the bar lines before you play.*

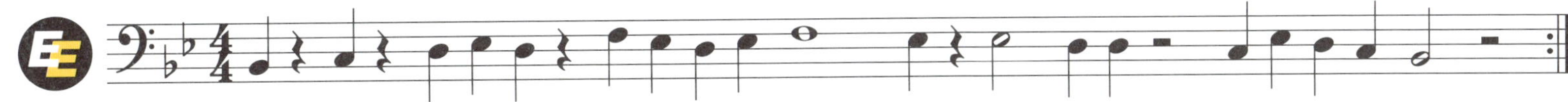

Fermata 𝄐 Hold the note (or rest) longer than normal.

27. REACHING HIGHER – New Note

Practice long tones on each new note.

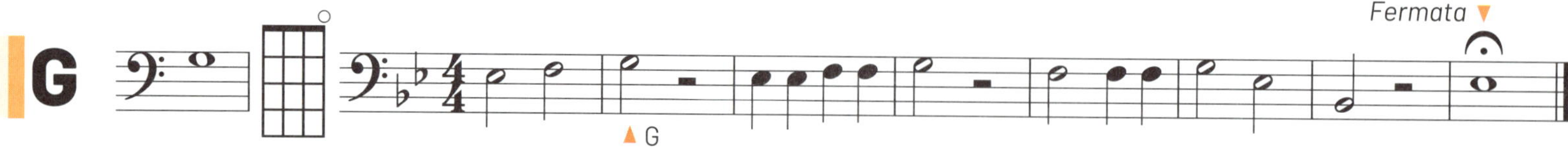

28. AU CLAIRE DE LA LUNE

French Folk Song

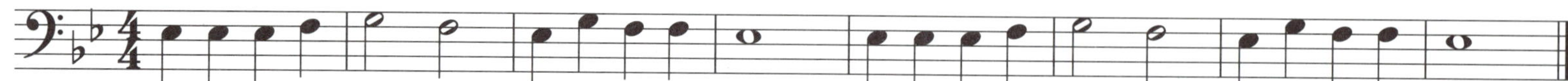

29. REMIX

THEORY

Harmony Two or more notes played together. Each combination forms a *chord.*

30. LONDON BRIDGE – Duet

English Folk Song

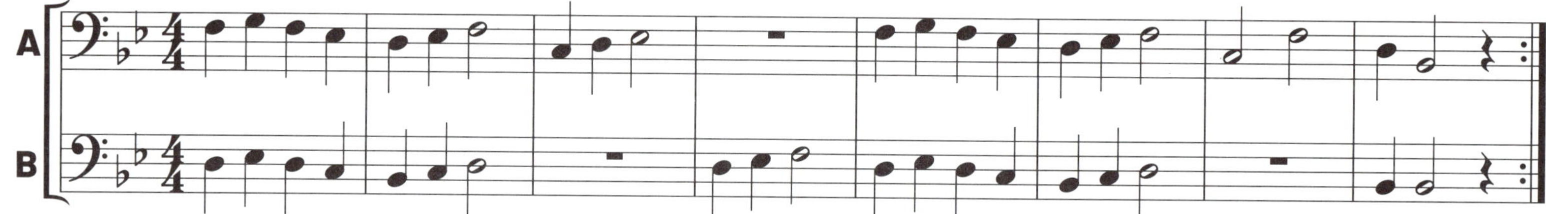

HISTORY

Austrian composer **Wolfgang Amadeus Mozart** (1756–1791) was a child prodigy who started playing professionally at age six, and lived during the time of the American Revolution. Mozart's music is melodic and imaginative. He wrote more than 600 compositions during his short life, including a piano piece based on the famous song, "Twinkle, Twinkle, Little Star."

31. A MOZART MELODY

Adaptation

32. ESSENTIAL ELEMENTS QUIZ

Draw these symbols where they belong and write in the note names before you play:

33. DEEP POCKETS – New Note

34. DOODLE ALL DAY

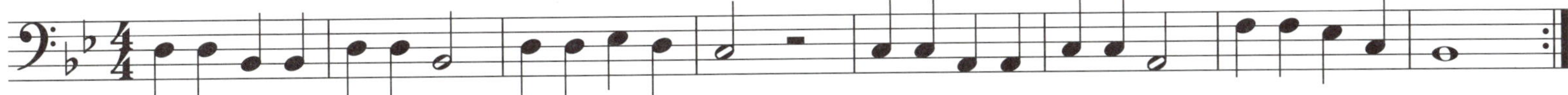

35. JUMP ROPE

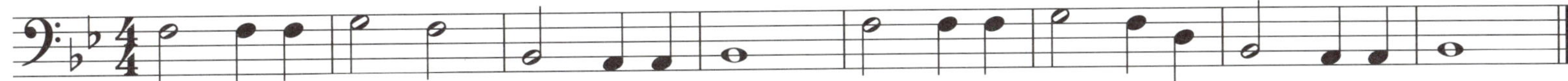

Pick-Up Notes One or more notes that come before the first full measure.
The beats of Pick-Up Notes are subtracted from the last measure.

36. A-TISKET, A-TASKET

Dynamics *f* – *forte* (play loudly) *mf* – *mezzo forte* (play moderately loud) *p* – *piano* (play softly)

37. LOUD AND SOFT

38. JINGLE BELLS *Always strive for consistent, even sound.*

Traditional Hanukkah Song

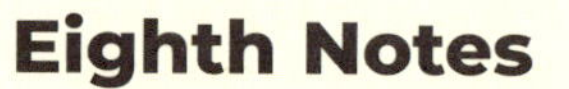

Eighth Notes

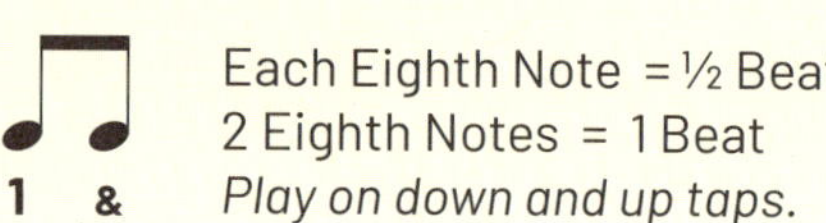

Two or more Eighth Notes have a *beam* across the stems.

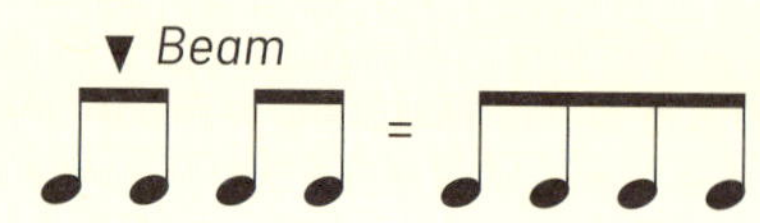

40. RHYTHM RAP *Clap the rhythm while counting and tapping.*

41. EIGHTH NOTE JAM

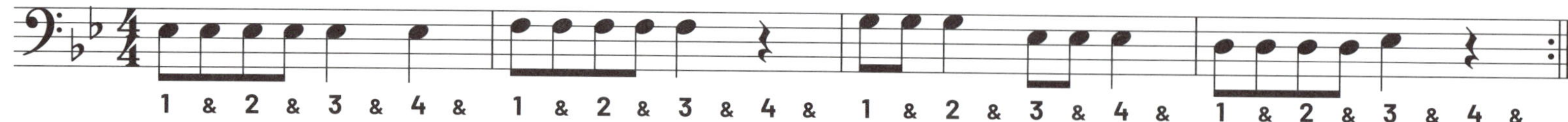

42. SKIP TO MY LOU

American Folk Song

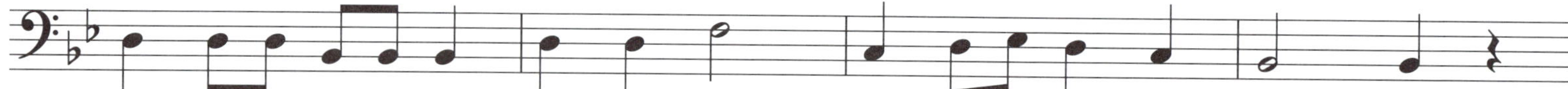

43. LONG, LONG AGO

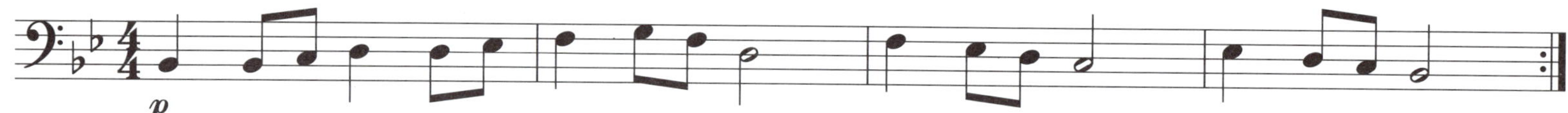

44. CANDY MOUNTAIN ROCK

HISTORY

Italian composer **Gioachino Rossini** (1792–1868) began composing as a teenager and was very proficient on the piano, viola and horn. He wrote "William Tell" at age 37 as the last of his forty operas, and its familiar theme is still heard today on radio and television.

45. ESSENTIAL ELEMENTS QUIZ – WILLIAM TELL

Gioachino Rossini

2/4 Time Signature

= **2 beats** per measure
= **Quarter** note gets one beat

Conducting

Practice conducting this two-beat pattern.

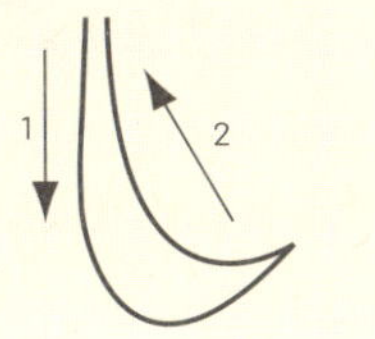

46. RHYTHM RAP

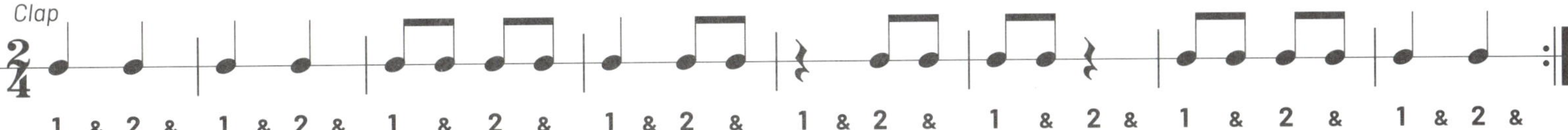

47. TWO BY TWO

Tempo Markings

Tempo is the speed of music. Tempo markings are usually written above the staff, in Italian.
Allegro – Fast tempo **Moderato** – Medium tempo **Andante** – Slower walking tempo

48. HIGH SCHOOL CADETS – March

John Philip Sousa

49. HEY, HO! NOBODY'S HOME – New Note

Dynamics

Crescendo (gradually louder) *Decrescendo* or *Diminuendo* (gradually softer)

50. CLAP THE DYNAMICS

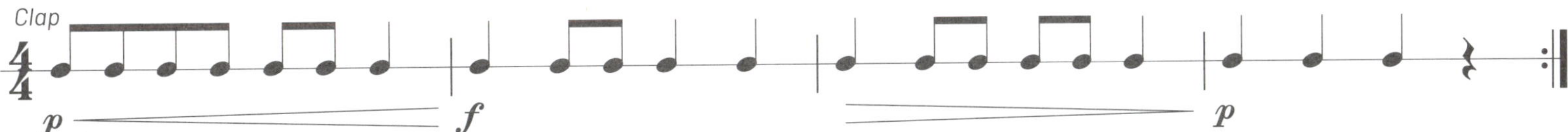

51. PLAY THE DYNAMICS

Looking for some more fun music to play?
See the inside front cover for instructions on accessing recent popular Bonus Songs.

PERFORMANCE SPOTLIGHT

52. PERFORMANCE WARM-UPS

TONE BUILDER

RHYTHM ETUDE

RHYTHM RAP

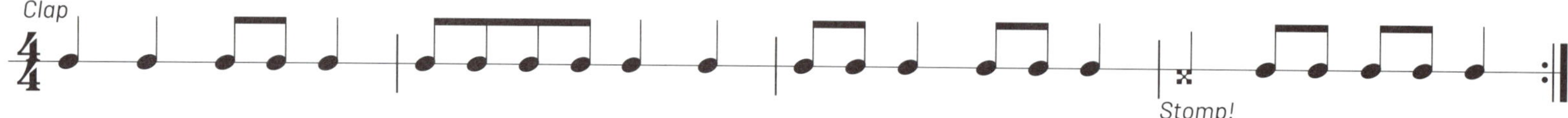

CHORALE

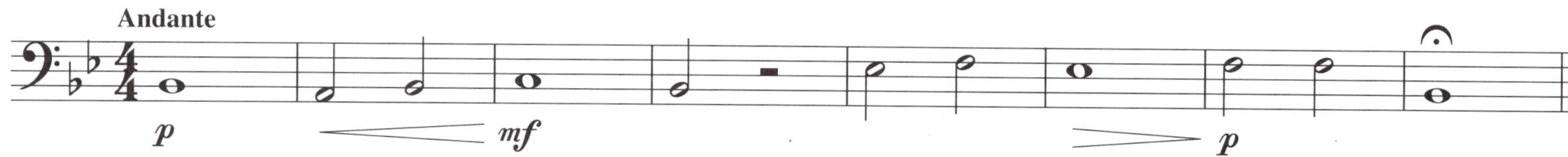

53. AURA LEE – Duet or Band Arrangement

(Part A = Melody, Part B = Harmony)

George R. Poulton

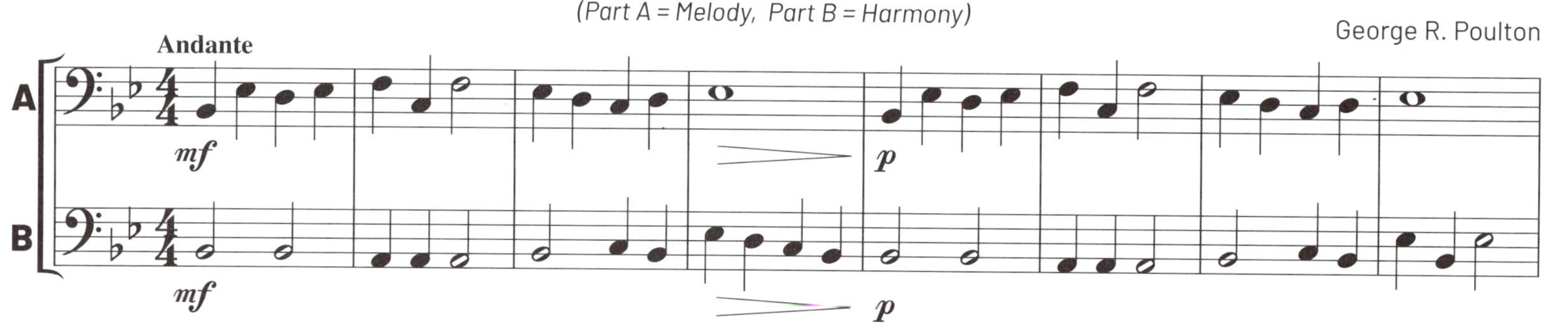

54. FRÈRE JACQUES – Round *(When group A reaches ②, group B begins at ①)*

French Folk Song

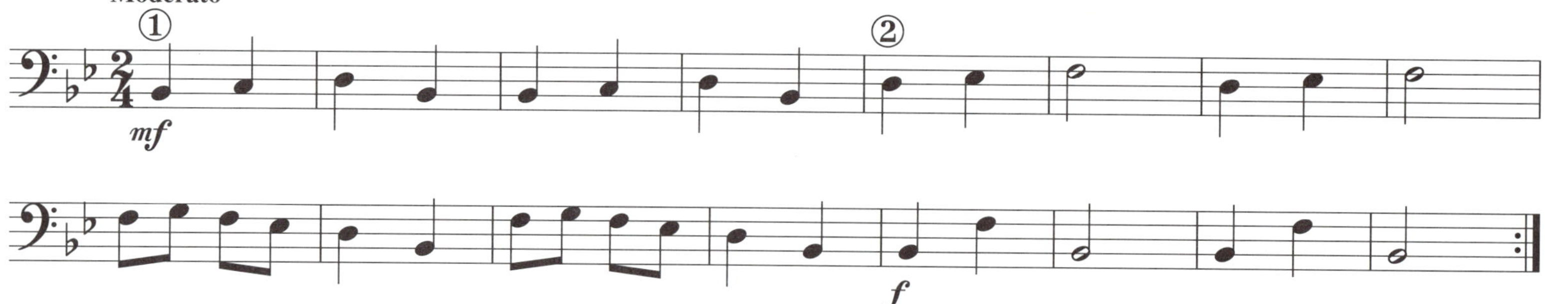

PERFORMANCE SPOTLIGHT

Tie

A curved line connecting notes of the same pitch.
Play one note for the combined counts of the tied notes.

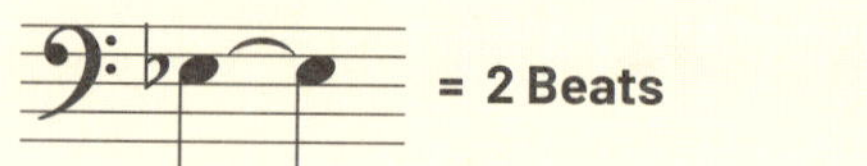

59. FIT TO BE TIED

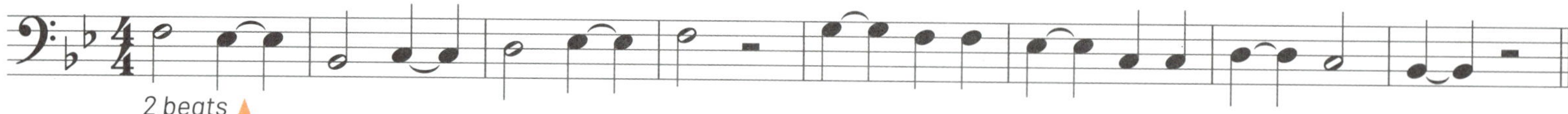

60. ALOUETTE

French-Canadian Folk Song

Dotted Half Note

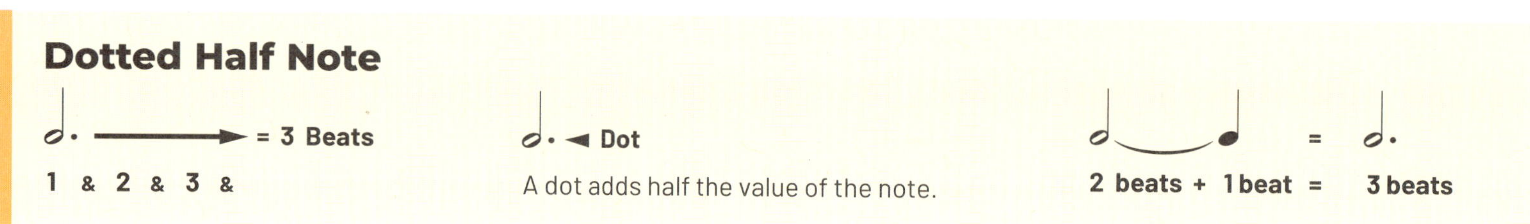

A dot adds half the value of the note.

61. ALOUETTE – THE SEQUEL

French-Canadian Folk Song

62. IT'S RAINING

63. NEW DIRECTIONS

64. THE NOBLES

65. ESSENTIAL ELEMENTS QUIZ

$\frac{3}{4}$ Time Signature

3/4 = **3 beats** per measure
= **Quarter** note gets one beat

Conducting

Practice conducting this three-beat pattern.

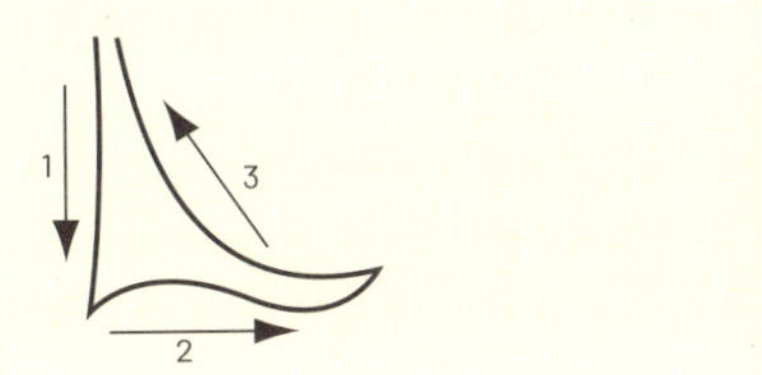

THEORY

66. RHYTHM RAP

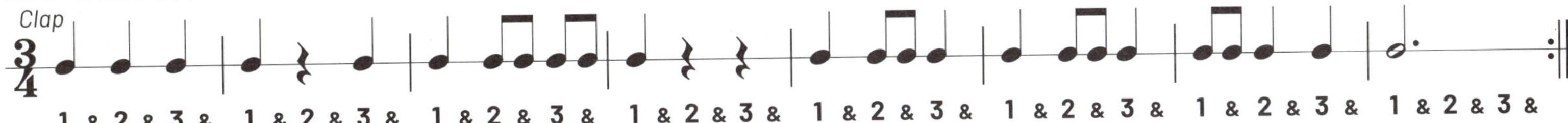

67. THREE BEAT JAM

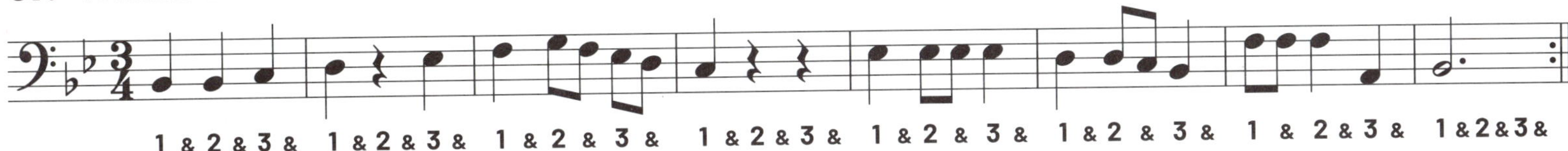

68. BARCAROLLE

Jacques Offenbach

Moderato

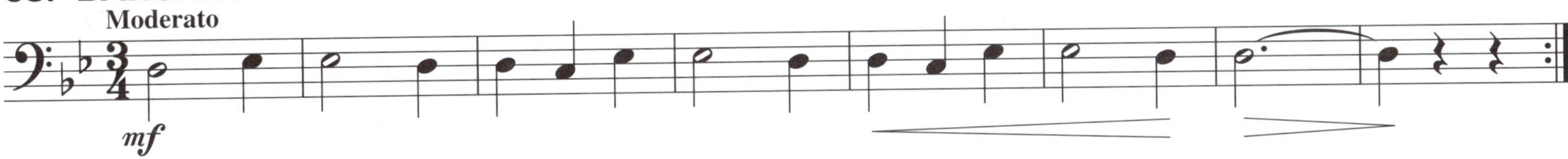

Norwegian composer **Edvard Grieg** (1843–1907) wrote *Peer Gynt Suite* for a play by Henrik Ibsen in 1875, the year before the telephone was invented by Alexander Graham Bell. "Morning" is a melody from *Peer Gynt Suite*. Music used in plays, or in films and television, is called **incidental music**.

HISTORY

69. MORNING (from Peer Gynt)

Edvard Grieg

Andante

Accent Emphasize the note.

70. ACCENT YOUR TALENT

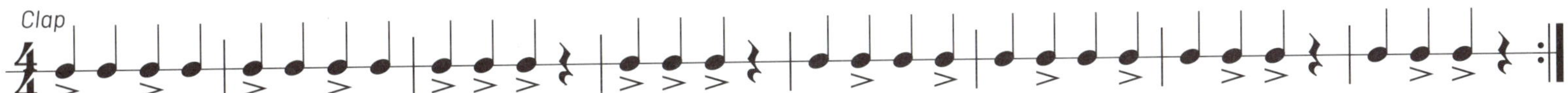

Latin American music has its roots in the African, Native American, Spanish and Portuguese cultures. This diverse music features lively accompaniments by drums and other percussion instruments such as maracas and claves. Music from Latin America continues to influence jazz, classical and popular styles of music. "Chiapanecas" is a popular children's dance and game song.

71. MEXICAN CLAPPING SONG ("Chiapanecas")

Latin American Folk Song

72. ESSENTIAL CREATIVITY

Compose your own music for measures 3 and 4 using this rhythm:

THEORY

Accidental

Any sharp, flat or natural sign which appears in the music without being in the key signature is called an **accidental**.

Flat ♭

A **flat** sign lowers the pitch of a note by a half-step. The note A-flat sounds a half-step below A, and all A's become A-flats for the rest of the measure where they occur.

73. HOT MUFFINS – New Note

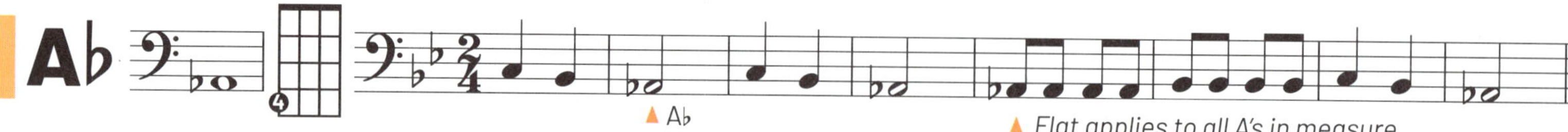

74. COSSACK DANCE

75. BASIC BLUES – New Note

THEORY

New Key Signature

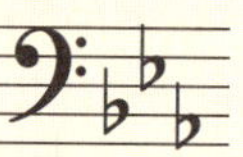

This Key Signature indicates the *Key of E♭* – play all B's as B-flats, all E's as E-flats, and all A's as A-flats.

1st & 2nd Endings

Play through the 1st Ending. Then play the repeated section of music, **skipping** the 1st Ending and playing the 2nd Ending.

76. HIGH FLYING

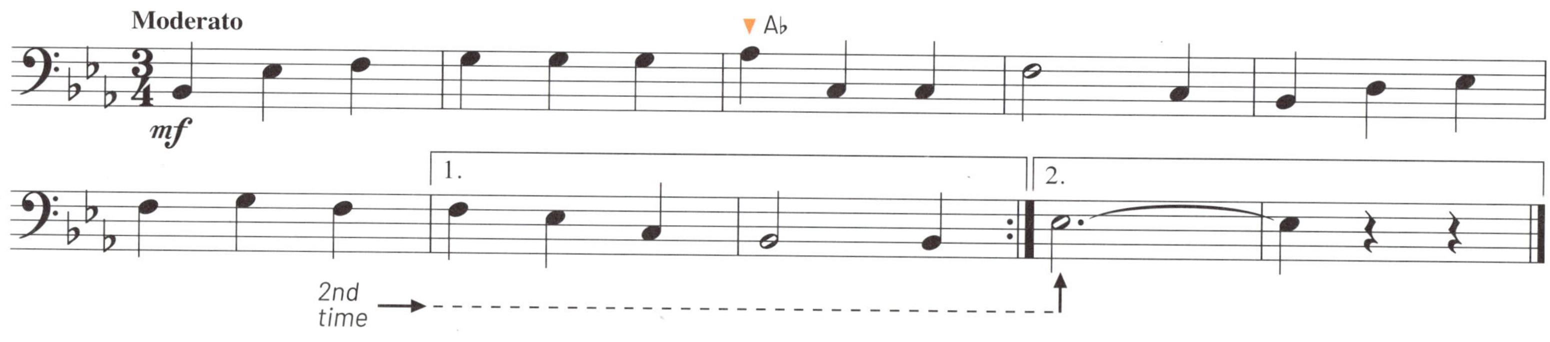

HISTORY

Japanese folk music actually has its origins in ancient China. "Sakura, Sakura" was performed on instruments such as the **koto**, a 13-string instrument that is more than 4000 years old, and the **shakuhachi** or bamboo flute. The unique sound of this ancient Japanese melody results from the pentatonic (or five-note) sequence used in this tonal system.

77. SAKURA, SAKURA – Band Arrangement

Japanese Folk Song
Arr. by John Higgins

78. UP ON A HOUSETOP

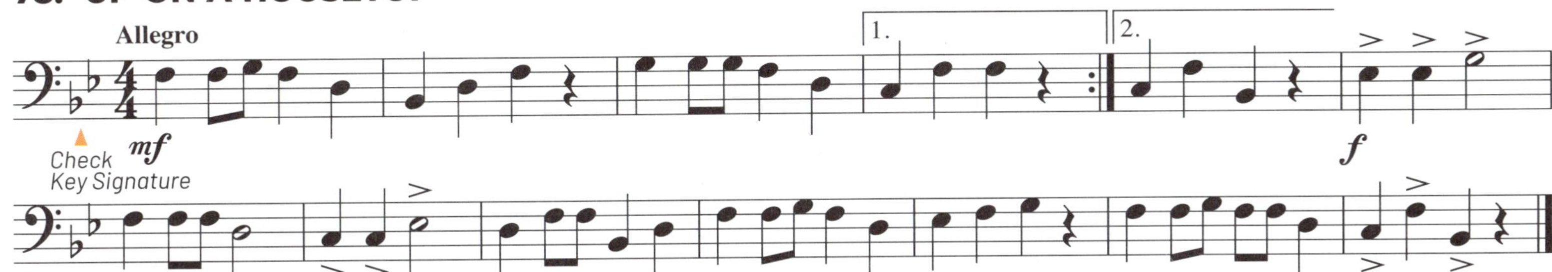

79. JOLLY OLD ST. NICK – Duet

See page 9 for additional holiday music, MY DREYDL and JINGLE BELLS.

80. THE BIG AIRSTREAM – New Note

B♭

81. WALTZ THEME (THE MERRY WIDOW WALTZ)

Franz Lehar

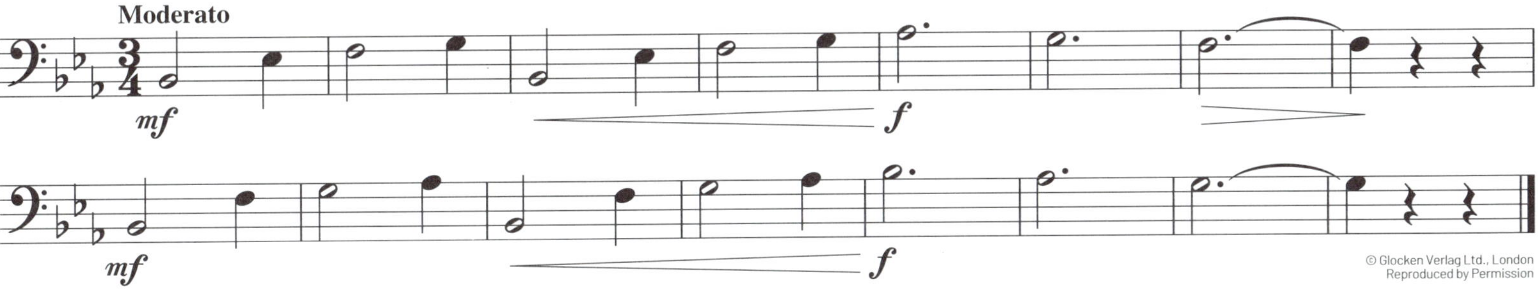

82. AIR TIME

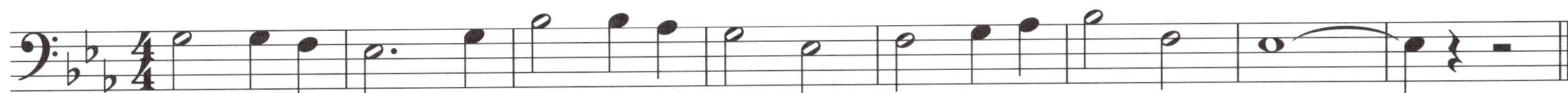

83. DOWN BY THE STATION

84. ESSENTIAL ELEMENTS QUIZ

85. ESSENTIAL CREATIVITY *Using these notes, improvise your own rhythms:*

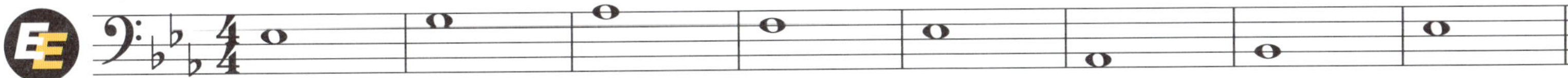

DAILY WARM-UPS

WORK-OUTS FOR TONE & TECHNIQUE

86. TONE BUILDER

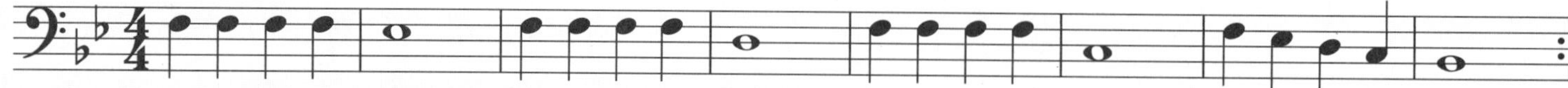

87. RHYTHM BUILDER

88. TECHNIQUE TRAX

89. CHORALE *(Adapted from Cantata 147)*

Johann Sebastian Bach

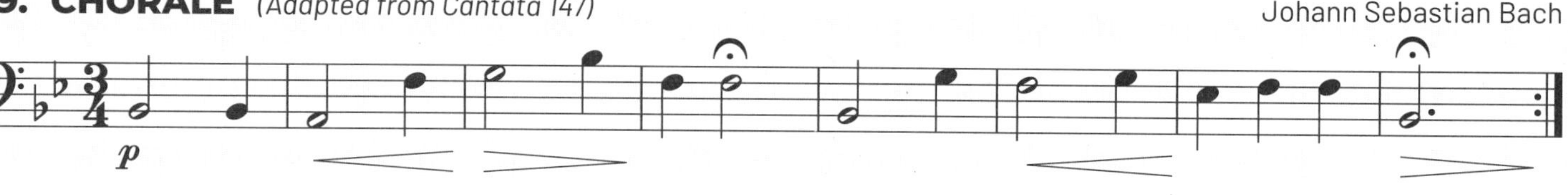

THEORY

Theme and Variations

A musical form featuring a **theme**, or primary melody, followed by **variations**, or altered versions of the theme.

90. VARIATIONS ON A FAMILIAR THEME

D.C. al Fine

At the **D.C. al Fine** play again from the beginning, stopping at **Fine** *(fee'- nay)*. **D.C.** is the abbreviation for **Da Capo**, or "to the beginning," and **Fine** means "the end."

91. BANANA BOAT SONG

Caribbean Folk Song

Natural ♮

A **natural** sign cancels a flat (♭) or sharp (♯) and remains in effect for the entire measure.

THEORY

92. RAZOR'S EDGE – New Note

93. THE MUSIC BOX

African-American spirituals originated in the 1700's, midway through the period of slavery in the United States. One of the largest categories of true American folk music, these primarily religious songs were sung and passed on for generations without being written down. The first collection of spirituals was published in 1867, four years after The Emancipation Proclamation was signed into law.

HISTORY

94. EZEKIEL SAW THE WHEEL

African-American Spiritual

95. SMOOTH OPERATOR

96. GLIDING ALONG

Ragtime is an American music style that was popular from the 1890's until the time of World War I. This early form of jazz brought fame to pianists like "Jelly Roll" Morton and Scott Joplin, who wrote "The Entertainer" and "Maple Leaf Rag." Surprisingly, the style was incorporated into some orchestral music by Igor Stravinsky and Claude Debussy. The trombones now learn to play a *glissando*, a technique used in ragtime and other styles of music.

HISTORY

97. TROMBONE RAG

98. ESSENTIAL ELEMENTS QUIZ

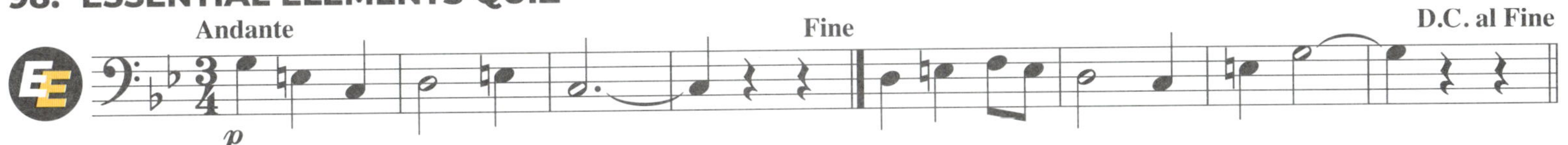

99. TAKE THE LEAD – New Note

THEORY

Phrase A musical "sentence" which is often 2 or 4 measures long.

100. THE COLD WIND

101. PHRASEOLOGY

THEORY

New Key Signature

This **Key Signature** indicates the *Key of F* – play all B's as B-flats.

Multiple Measure Rest

The number above the staff tells you how many full measures to rest. Count each measure of rest in sequence:

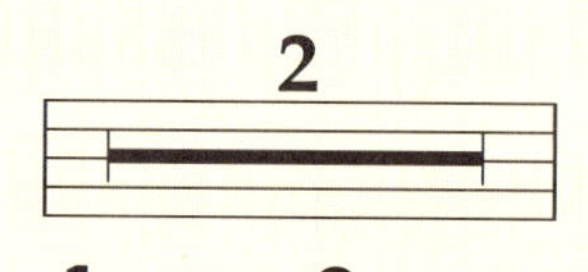

1-2-3-4 **2**-2-3-4

102. SATIN LATIN

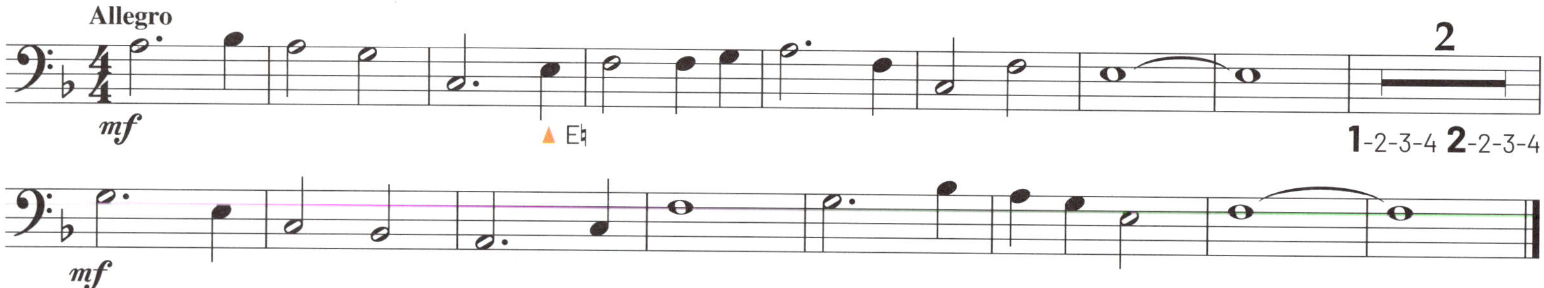

HISTORY

German composer **Johann Sebastian Bach** (1685–1750) was part of a large family of famous musicians and became the most recognized composer of the Baroque era. Beginning as a choir member, Bach soon became an organist, a teacher, and a prolific composer, writing more than 600 masterworks. This *Minuet*, or dance in 3/4 time, was written as a teaching piece for use with an early form of the piano.

103. MINUET – Duet

Johann Sebastian Bach

104. ESSENTIAL CREATIVITY

This melody can be played in 3/4 or 4/4. Pencil in either time signature, draw the bar lines and play. Now erase the bar lines and try the other time signature. Do the phrases sound different?

105. NATURALLY

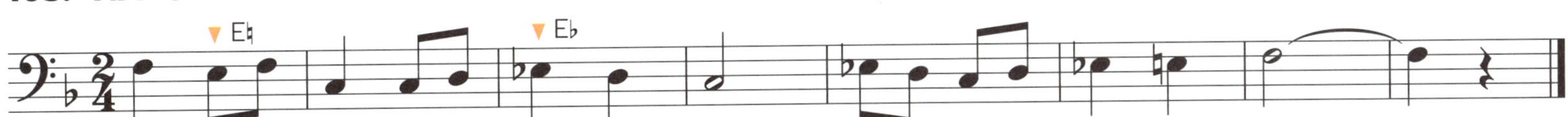

Austrian composer **Franz Peter Schubert** (1797–1828) lived a shorter life than any other great composer, but he created an incredible amount of music: more than 600 art-songs (concert music for voice and accompaniment), ten symphonies, chamber music, operas, choral works and piano pieces. His "March Militaire" was originally a piano duet.

HISTORY

106. MARCH MILITAIRE

Franz Schubert

107. THE FLAT ZONE – New Note

D♭

108. ON TOP OF OLD SMOKEY

American Folk Song

Boogie-woogie is a style of the **blues**, and it was first recorded by pianist Clarence "Pine Top" Smith in 1928, one year after Charles Lindbergh's solo flight across the Atlantic. A form of jazz, blues music features altered notes and is usually written in 12-measure verses, like "Bottom Bass Boogie."

HISTORY

109. BOTTOM BASS BOOGIE – Duet

Dotted Quarter & Eighth Notes
= 2 Beats
1 & 2 &
A dot adds half the value of the quarter note.
1 & 2 &
A single eighth note has a flag on the stem.
110. RHYTHM RAP
Clap
1 & 2 & 3 & 4 & 1 & 2 & 3 & 4 & 1 & 2 & 3 & 4 & 1 & 2 & 3 & 4 &
111. THE DOT ALWAYS COUNTS
1 & 2 & 3 & 4 & 1 & 2 & 3 & 4 & 1 & 2 & 3 & 4 & 1 & 2 & 3 & 4 &
112. ALL THROUGH THE NIGHT
Fine
D.C. al Fine
mf
p
113. SEA CHANTY
English Folk Song
Moderato
f
mf
f
114. SCARBOROUGH FAIR
English Folk Song
Andante
mf
f
mf
p
115. RHYTHM RAP
Clap
1 & 2 & 3 & 4 & 1 & 2 & 3 & 4 & 1 & 2 & 3 & 4 & 1 & 2 & 3 & 4 &
116. THE TURNAROUND
1 & 2 & 3 & 4 & 1 & 2 & 3 & 4 & 1 & 2 & 3 & 4 & 1 & 2 & 3 & 4 &
117. ESSENTIAL ELEMENTS QUIZ – AULD LANG SYNE
Scottish Folk Song
EE
Andante
mf
Check Rhythm
f

PERFORMANCE SPOTLIGHT

Solo with Piano Accompaniment

You can perform this solo with or without a piano accompanist. Play it for the band, the school or your family. It is part of **Symphony No. 9 ("From The New World")** by Czech composer **Antonin Dvorák** (1841–1904). He wrote it while visiting America in 1893, and was inspired to include melodies from American folksongs and spirituals. This is the **Largo** (or "very slow tempo") theme.

118. THEME FROM "NEW WORLD SYMPHONY"

Antonin Dvorák

Great musicians give encouragement to fellow performers. On this page, clarinetists learn their instruments' upper register in the "Grenadilla Gorilla Jumps" (named after the grenadilla wood used to make clarinets). Brass players learn lip slurs, a new warm-up pattern. The success of your band depends on everyone's effort and encouragement.

119. GRENADILLA GORILLA JUMP No. 1

120. JUMPIN' UP AND DOWN

121. GRENADILLA GORILLA JUMP No. 2

122. JUMPIN' FOR JOY

123. GRENADILLA GORILLA JUMP No. 3

124. JUMPIN' JACKS

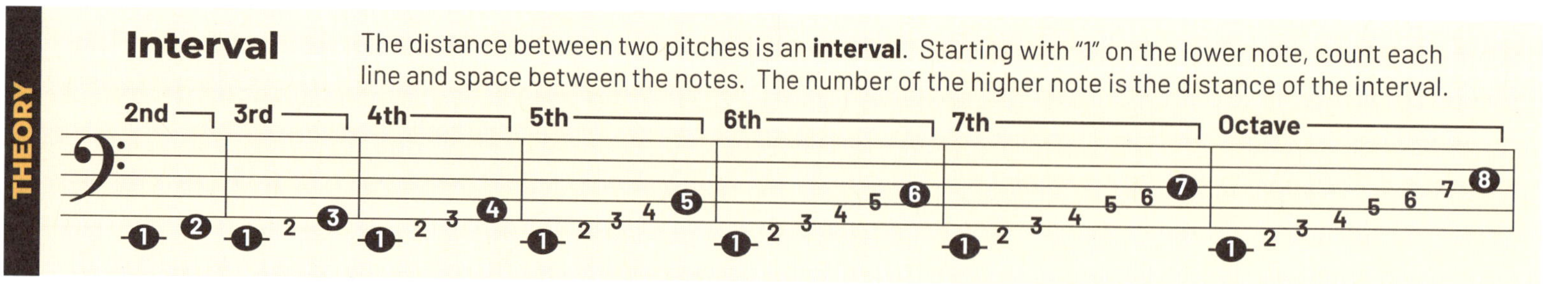

Interval The distance between two pitches is an **interval**. Starting with "1" on the lower note, count each line and space between the notes. The number of the higher note is the distance of the interval.

125. ESSENTIAL ELEMENTS QUIZ

Write in the numbers of the intervals, counting up from the lower notes.

Additional bonus songs are available online. See the inside front cover for details.

126. GRENADILLA GORILLA JUMP No. 4

127. THREE IS THE COUNT

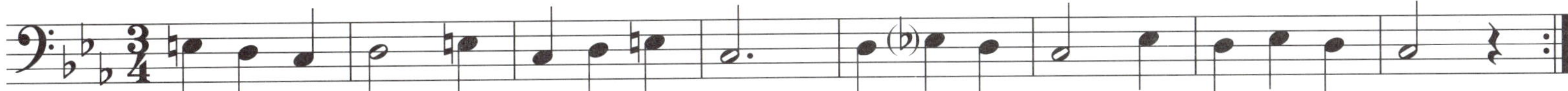

128. GRENADILLA GORILLA JUMP No. 5

129. TECHNIQUE TRAX

130. CROSSING OVER – New Note

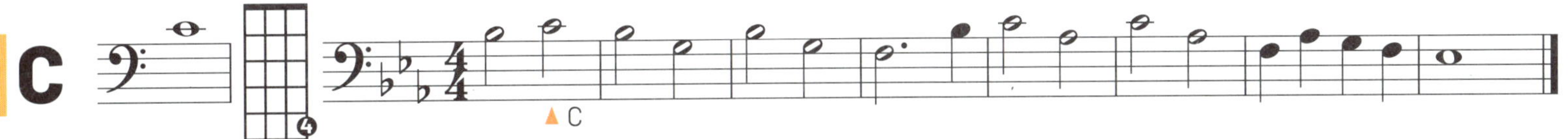

Trio A **trio** is a composition with three parts played together. Practice this trio with two other players and listen for 3-part harmony.

131. KUM BAH YAH – Trio *Always check the key signature.* African Folk Song

Repeat Signs

Repeat the section of music enclosed by the **repeat signs**. *(If 1st and 2nd endings are used, they are played as usual – but go back only to the first repeat sign, not to the beginning.)*

132. MICHAEL ROW THE BOAT ASHORE

African-American Spiritual

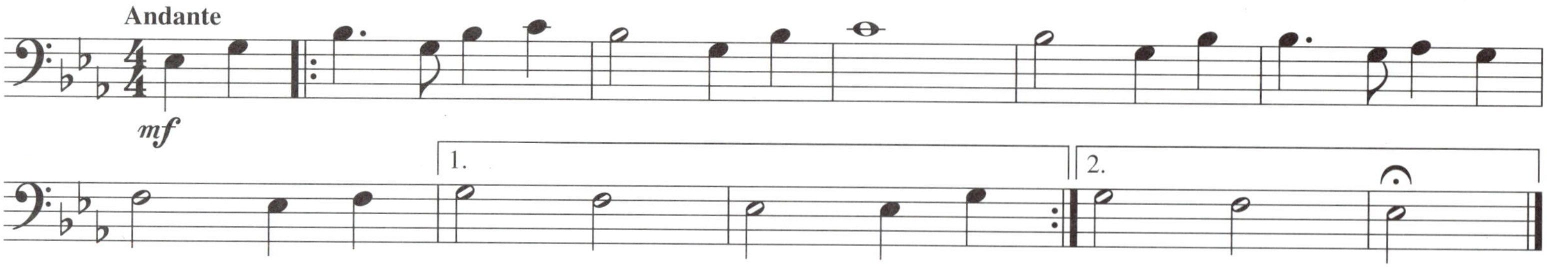

Andante

mf

1. 2.

133. AUSTRIAN WALTZ

Austrian Folk Song

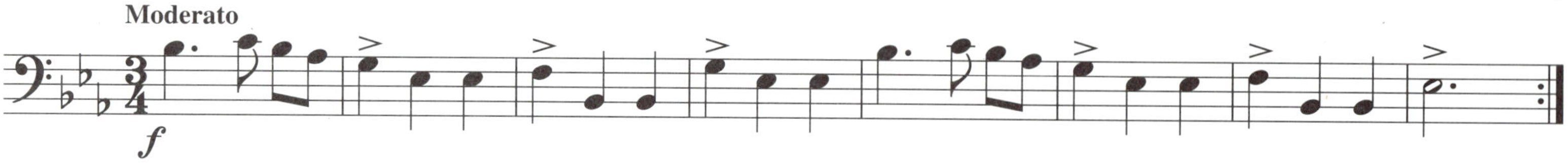

Moderato

f

134. BOTANY BAY

Australian Folk Song

Allegro

mf *f* *mf*

THEORY

C Time Signature

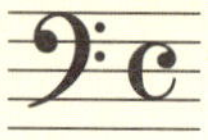

C = **Common Time** (Same as $\frac{4}{4}$)

Conducting

Practice conducting this four-beat pattern.

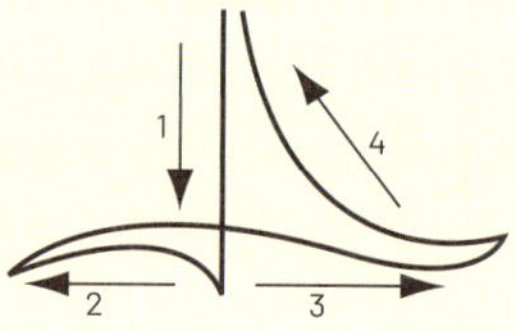

1 2 3 4

135. TECHNIQUE TRAX

Practice at all dynamic levels.

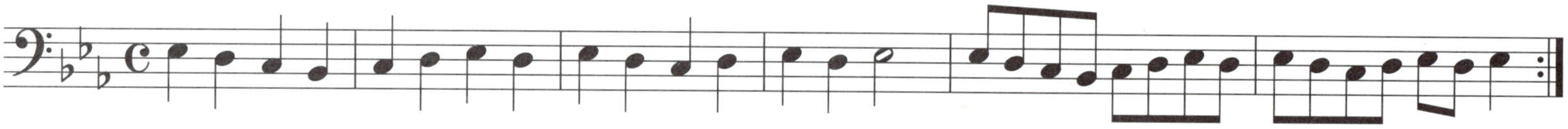

136. FINLANDIA

Jean Sibelius

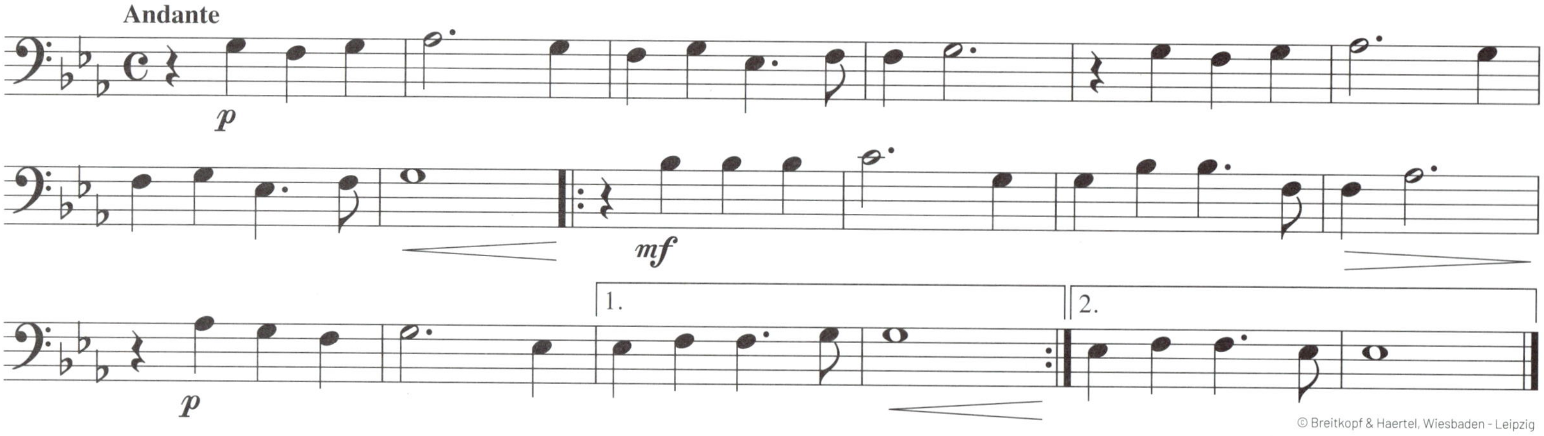

Andante

p *mf* *p*

1. 2.

137. ESSENTIAL CREATIVITY

Create your own variations by penciling in a dot and a flag to change the rhythm of any measure from ♩ ♩ *to* ♩. ♪

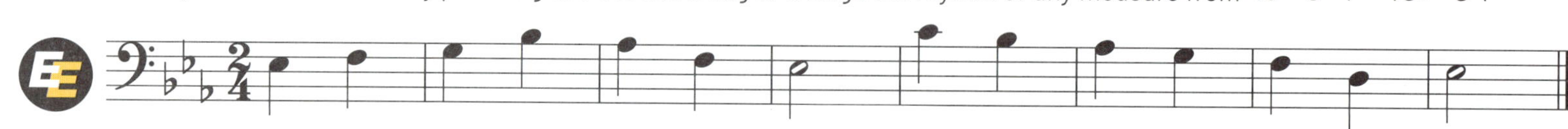

138. EASY GORILLA JUMPS

139. TECHNIQUE TRAX *Always check the key signature.*

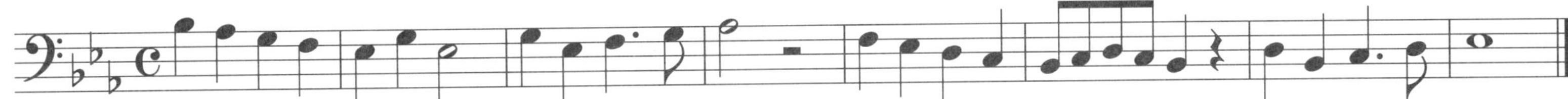

140. MORE TECHNIQUE TRAX

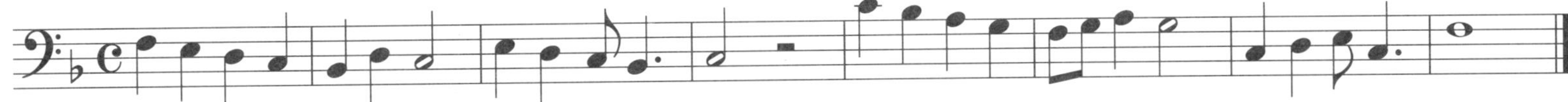

141. GERMAN FOLK SONG

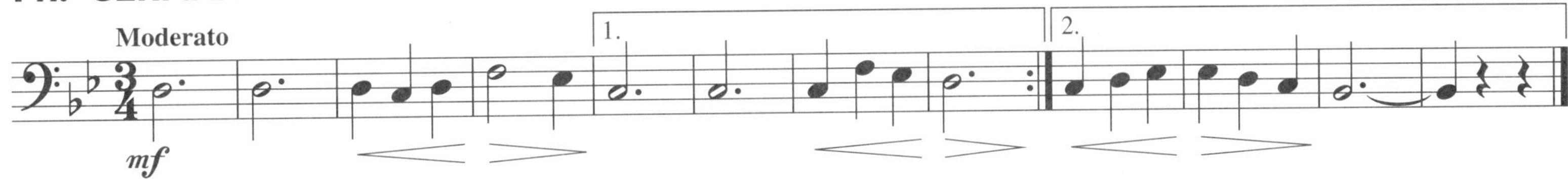

142. THE SAINTS GO MARCHIN' AGAIN

James Black and Katherine Purvis

143. LOWLAND GORILLA WALK

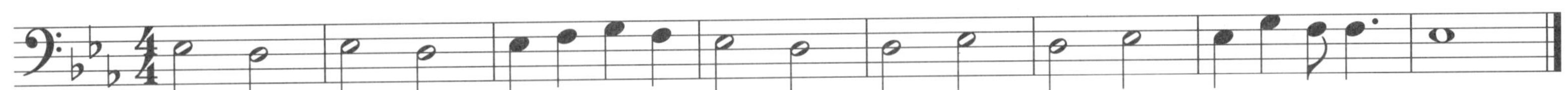

144. SMOOTH SAILING

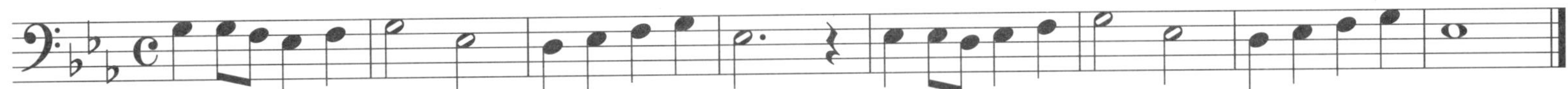

145. MORE GORILLA JUMPS

146. FULL COVERAGE

THEORY — Scale

A **scale** is a sequence of notes in ascending or descending order. Like a musical "ladder," each step is the next consecutive note in the key. This scale is in your Key of B♭ (two flats), so the top and bottom notes are both B♭'s. The interval between the B♭'s is an octave.

147. CONCERT B♭ SCALE

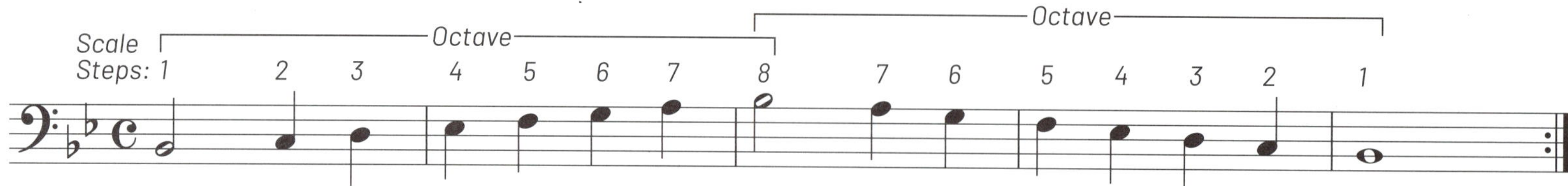

THEORY — Chord & Arpeggio

When two or more notes are played together, they form a **chord** or **harmony**. This B♭ chord is built from the 1st, 3rd and 5th steps of the B♭ scale. The 8th step is the same as the 1st, but it is an octave higher. An **arpeggio** is a "broken" chord whose notes are played individually.

148. IN HARMONY

Divide the notes of the chords between band members and play together. Does the arpeggio sound like a chord?

149. SCALE AND ARPEGGIO

HISTORY

Austrian composer **Franz Josef Haydn** (1732–1809) wrote 104 symphonies. Many of these works had nicknames and included brilliant, unique effects for their time. His *Symphony No. 94* was named "The Surprise Symphony" because the soft second movement included a sudden loud dynamic, intended to wake up an often sleepy audience. Pay special attention to dynamics when you play this famous theme.

150. THEME FROM "SURPRISE SYMPHONY"

Franz Josef Haydn

151. ESSENTIAL ELEMENTS QUIZ – THE STREETS OF LAREDO

American Folk Song

Write in the note names before you play.

PERFORMANCE SPOTLIGHT

152. SCHOOL SPIRIT – Band Arrangement

W.T. Purdy
Arr. by John Higgins

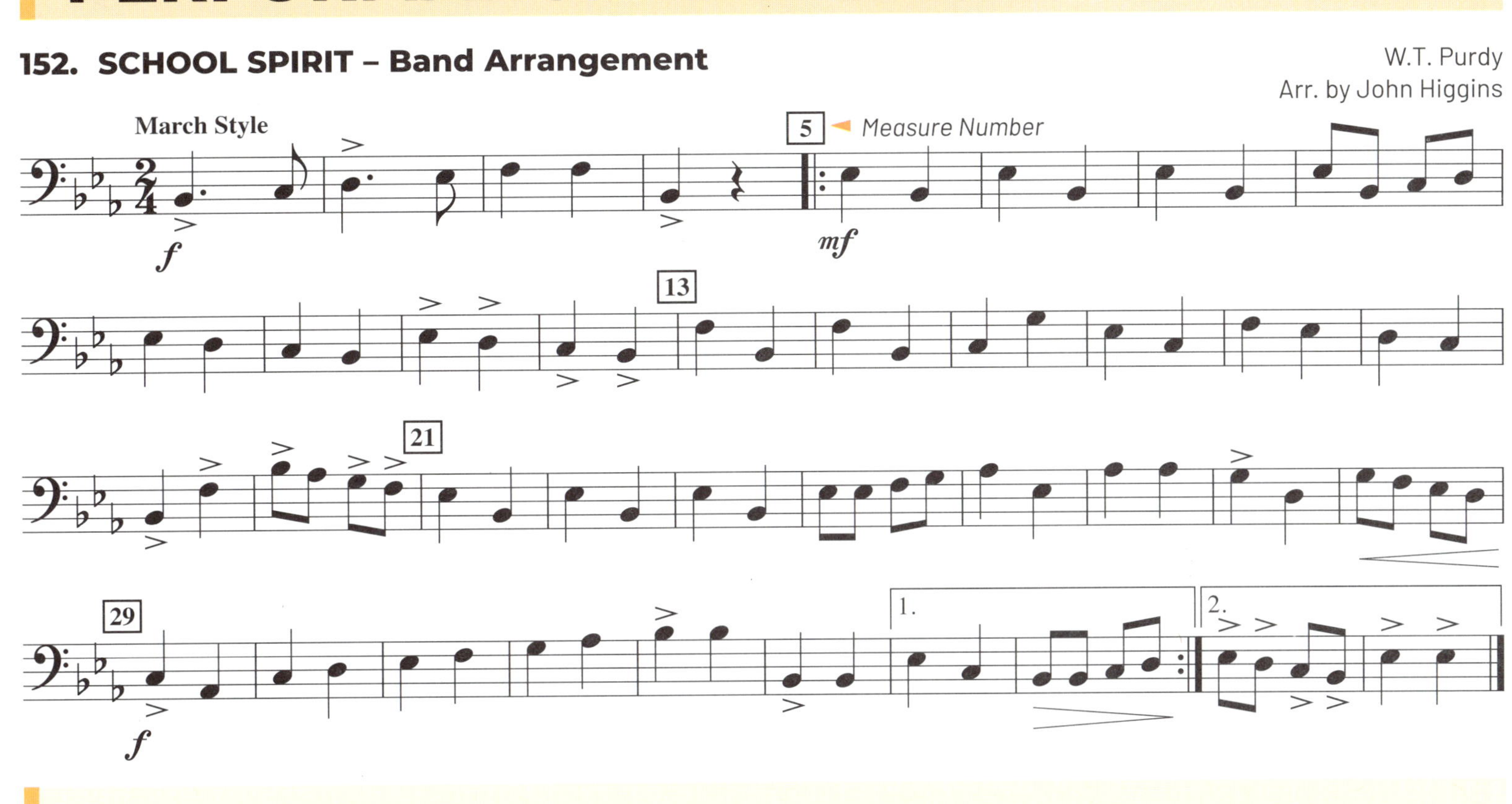

Soli When playing music marked **Soli**, you are part of a group "solo" or group feature. Listen carefully in "Carnival of Venice," and name the instruments that play the Soli part at each indicated measure number.

153. CARNIVAL OF VENICE – Band Arrangement

Julius Benedict
Arr. by John Higgins

Allegro

5

13 8

21 7

29

Soli

end Soli

37 7

45

DAILY WARM-UPS

WORK-OUTS FOR TONE & TECHNIQUE

154. RANGE AND FLEXIBILITY BUILDER

155. TECHNIQUE TRAX

156. CHORALE

Johann Sebastian Bach

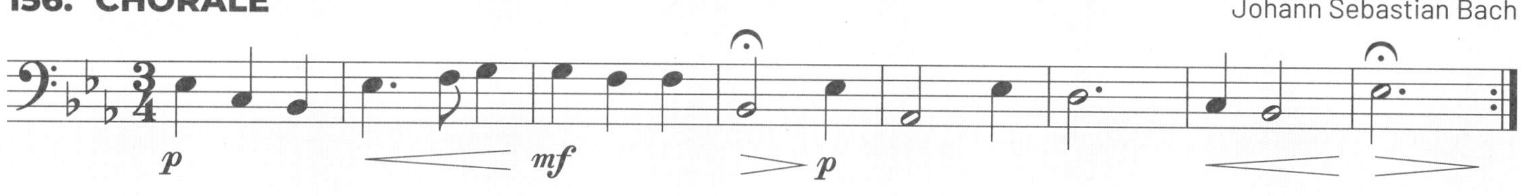

The traditional Hebrew melody "Hatikvah" has been Israel's national anthem since the nation's inception. At the Declaration of State in 1948, it was sung by the gathered assembly during the opening ceremony and played by members of the Palestine Symphony Orchestra at its conclusion.

157. HATIKVAH

Israeli National Anthem

Eighth Note & Eighth Rest

♪ = 1/2 beat of sound
𝄾 = 1/2 beat of silence

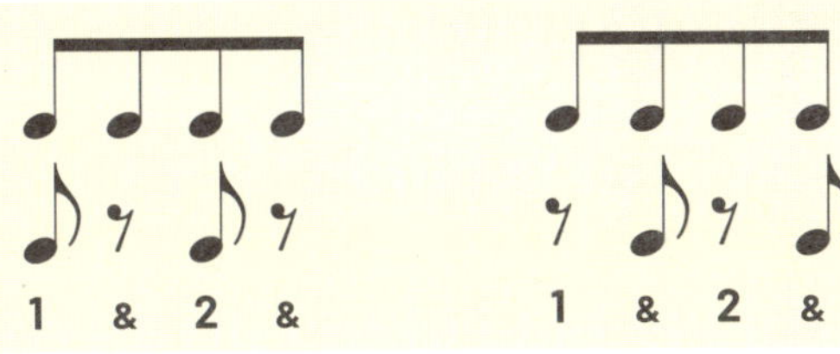

158. RHYTHM RAP

159. EIGHTH NOTE MARCH

160. MINUET

Johann Sebastian Bach

161. RHYTHM RAP

162. EIGHTH NOTES OFF THE BEAT

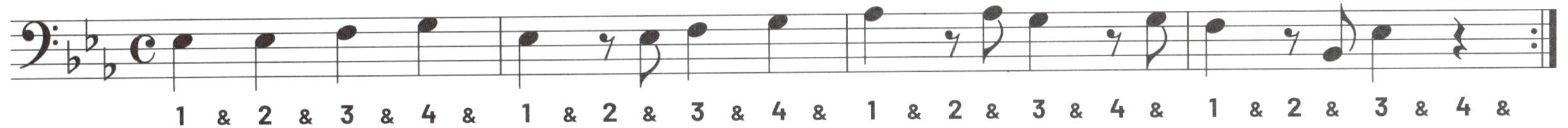

163. EIGHTH NOTE SCRAMBLE

164. ESSENTIAL ELEMENTS QUIZ

165. DANCING MELODY – New Note

HISTORY

American composer and conductor **John Philip Sousa** (1854-1932) wrote 136 marches. Known as "The March King," Sousa wrote *The Stars And Stripes Forever*, *Semper Fidelis*, *The Washington Post* and many other patriotic works. Sousa's band performed all over the country, and his fame helped boost the popularity of bands in America. Here is a melody from his famous *El Capitan* operetta and march.

166. EL CAPITAN

John Philip Sousa

HISTORY

"O Canada," formerly known as the "National Song," was first performed during 1880 in French Canada. Robert Stanley Weir translated the English language version in 1908, but it was not adopted as the national anthem of Canada until 1980, one hundred years after its premiere.

167. O CANADA

Calixa Lavallee,
l'Hon. Judge Routhier and Justice R.S. Weir

168. ESSENTIAL ELEMENTS QUIZ – METER MANIA

Count and clap before playing. Can you conduct this?

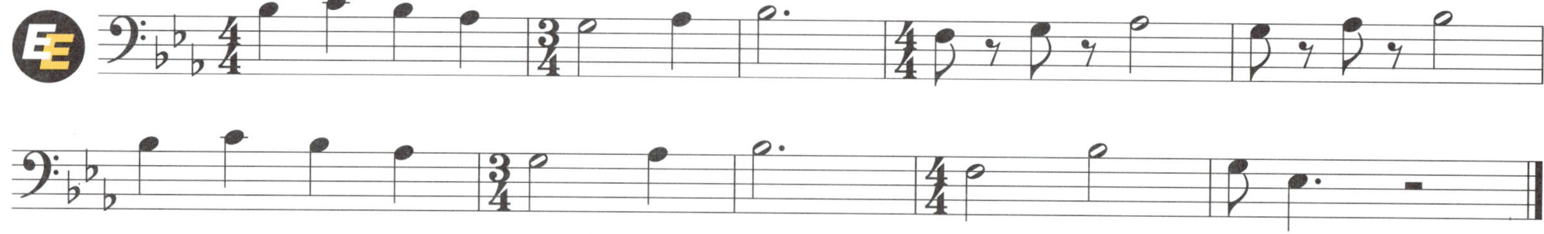

Enharmonics

Two notes that are written differently, but sound the same (and played with the same fingering) are called **enharmonics**. Your fingering chart on pages 46–47 shows the fingerings for the enharmonic notes on your instrument.

On a piano keyboard, each black key is both a flat and a sharp:

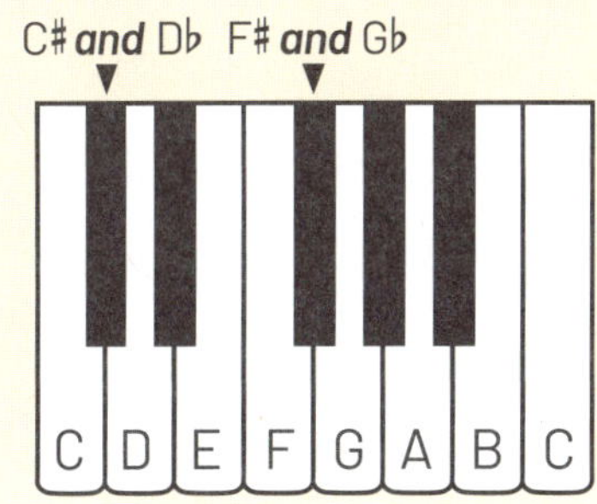

THEORY

169. SNAKE CHARMER

Enharmonic notes use the same fingering.

170. DARK SHADOWS

171. CLOSE ENCOUNTERS

Enharmonic notes use the same fingering.

172. MARCH SLAV

Peter Ilyich Tchaikovsky

173. NOTES IN DISGUISE

Chromatic Notes

Chromatic notes are altered with sharps, flats and natural signs which are not in the key signature. The smallest distance between two notes is a half-step, and a scale made up of consecutive half-steps is called a **chromatic scale**.

THEORY

174. HALF-STEPPIN'

HISTORY

French composer **Camille Saint-Saëns** (1835-1921) wrote music for virtually every medium: operas, suites, symphonies and chamber works. The "Egyptian Dance" is one of the main themes from his famous opera *Samson et Delilah*. The opera was written in the same year that Thomas Edison invented the phonograph—1877.

175. EGYPTIAN DANCE *Watch for enharmonics.*

Camille Saint-Saëns

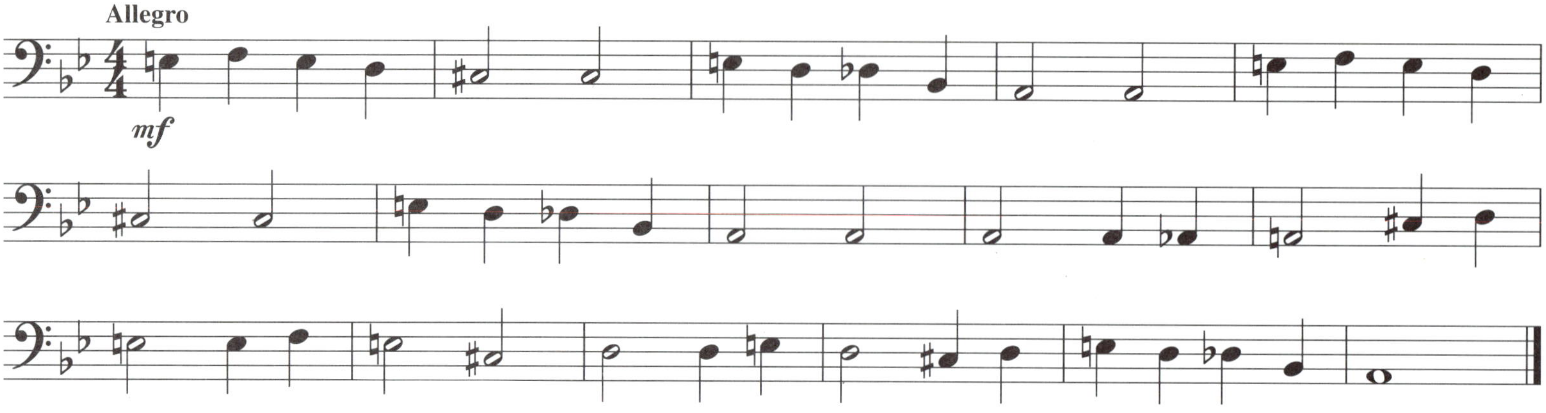
Allegro
mf

176. SILVER MOON BOAT

Chinese Folk Song

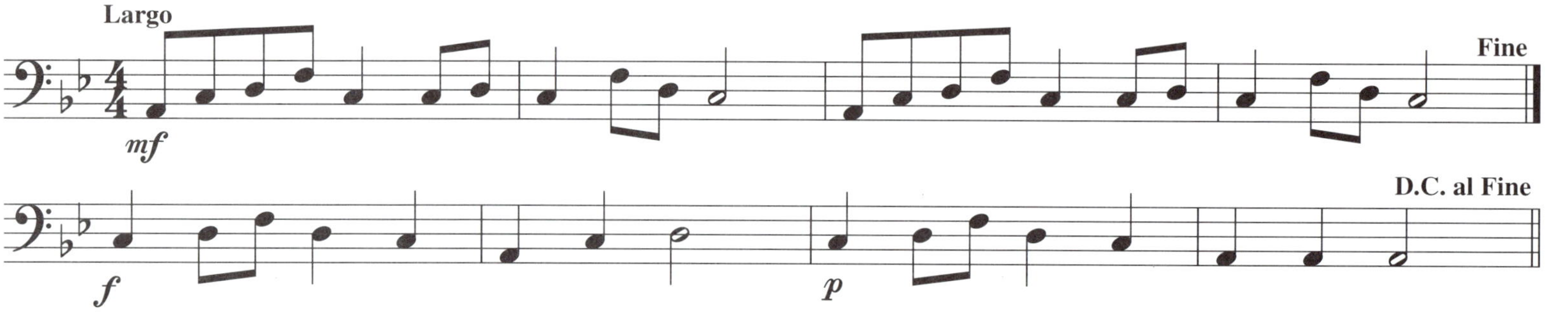
Largo
mf
Fine
D.C. al Fine
f
p

HISTORY

German composer **Ludwig van Beethoven** (1770-1827) is considered to be one of the world's greatest composers, despite becoming completely deaf in 1802. Although he could not hear his music the way we can, he could "hear" it in his mind. As a testament to his greatness, his *Symphony No. 9* (p. 13) was performed as the finale to the ceremony celebrating the reunification of Germany in 1990. This is the theme from his *Symphony No. 7*, second movement.

177. THEME FROM SYMPHONY NO. 7 – Duet

Ludwig van Beethoven

Allegro (moderately fast)
A
B
p
9
mf
1.
2.

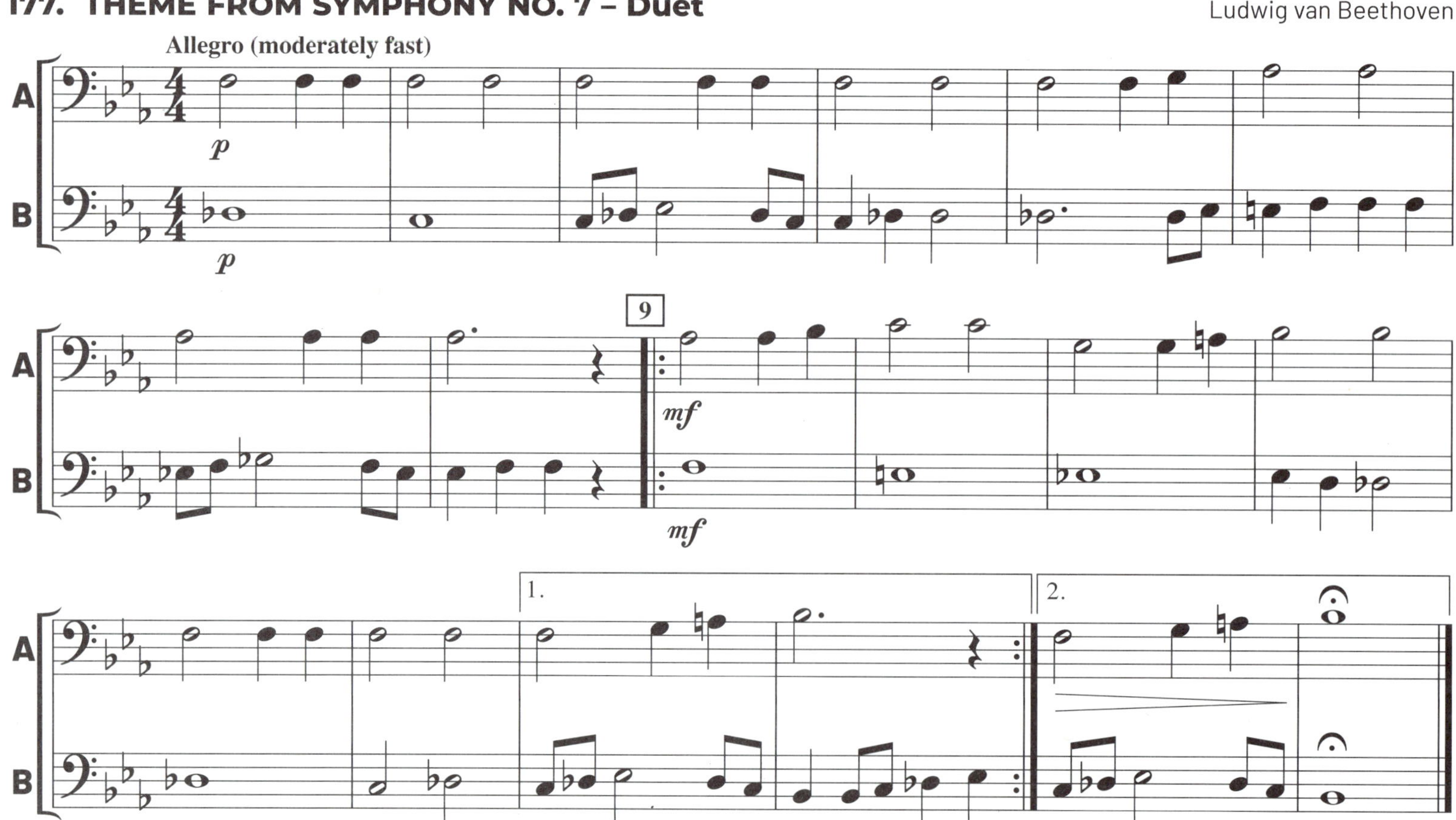

Russian composer **Peter Ilyich Tchaikovsky** (1840–1893) wrote six symphonies and hundreds of other works including *The Nutcracker* ballet. He was a master at writing brilliant settings of folk music, and his original melodies are among the most popular of all time. His *1812 Overture* and *Capriccio Italien* were both written in 1880, the year after Thomas Edison developed the practical electric light bulb.

HISTORY

Additional bonus songs are available online. See the inside front cover for details.

PERFORMANCE SPOTLIGHT

PERFORMANCE SPOTLIGHT

184. THEME FROM 1812 OVERTURE – Band Arrangement

Peter Ilyich Tchaikovsky
Arr. by John Higgins

Allegro

f p f p 10 18 4 mf f 26 34 42

PERFORMANCE SPOTLIGHT

Solo with Piano Accompaniment

Performing for an audience is an exciting part of being involved in music. This solo is based on *Symphony No. 1* by German composer **Johannes Brahms** (1833-1897). He completed his first symphony in 1876, the same year that the telephone was invented by Alexander Graham Bell. You and a piano accompanist can perform this for the band or at other school and community events.

185. THEME FROM SYMPHONY NO. 1 – Solo *(Concert E♭ version)*

Johannes Brahms
Arr. by John Higgins

DUETS

Here is an opportunity to get together with a friend and enjoy playing music. The other player does not have to play the same instrument as you. Try to exactly match each other's rhythm, pitch and tone quality. Eventually, it may begin to sound like the two parts are being played by one person! Later, try switching parts.

186. SWING LOW, SWEET CHARIOT – Duet

African-American Spiritual

RUBANK® SCALE AND ARPEGGIO STUDIES

KEY OF B♭ *In this key signature, play all B♭'s and E♭'s.*

1.

2.

3.

4.

KEY OF E♭ *In this key signature, play all B♭'s, E♭'s and A♭'s.*

1.

2.

3.

4.

RUBANK® SCALE AND ARPEGGIO STUDIES

RHYTHM STUDIES

RHYTHM STUDIES

CREATING MUSIC

THEORY

Composition

Composition is the art of writing original music. A composer often begins by creating a melody made up of individual **phrases**, like short musical "sentences." Some melodies have phrases that seem to answer or respond to "question" phrases, as in Beethoven's *Ode To Joy*. Play this melody and listen to how phrases 2 and 4 give slightly different answers to the same question (phrases 1 and 3).

1. ODE TO JOY

Ludwig van Beethoven

1. Question *2. Answer* *3. Question* *4. Answer*

2. Q. AND A. *Write your own "answer" phrases in this melody.*

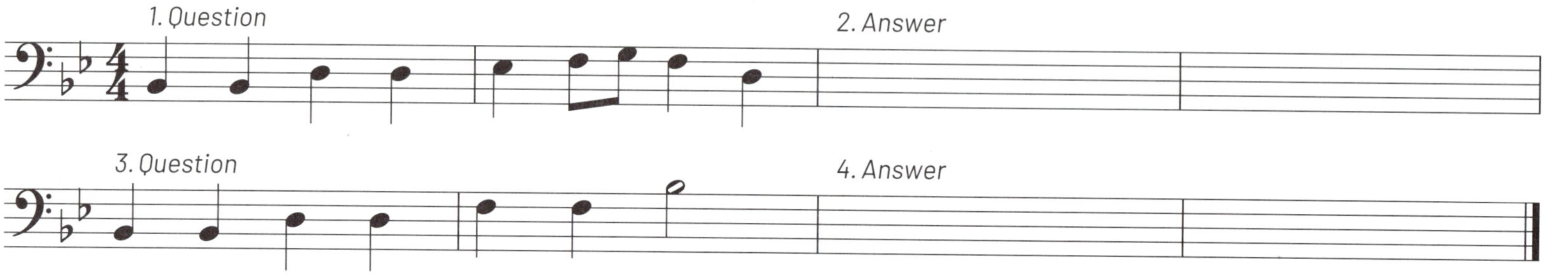

1. Question *2. Answer*

3. Question *4. Answer*

3. PHRASE BUILDERS *Write 4 different phrases using the rhythms below each staff.*

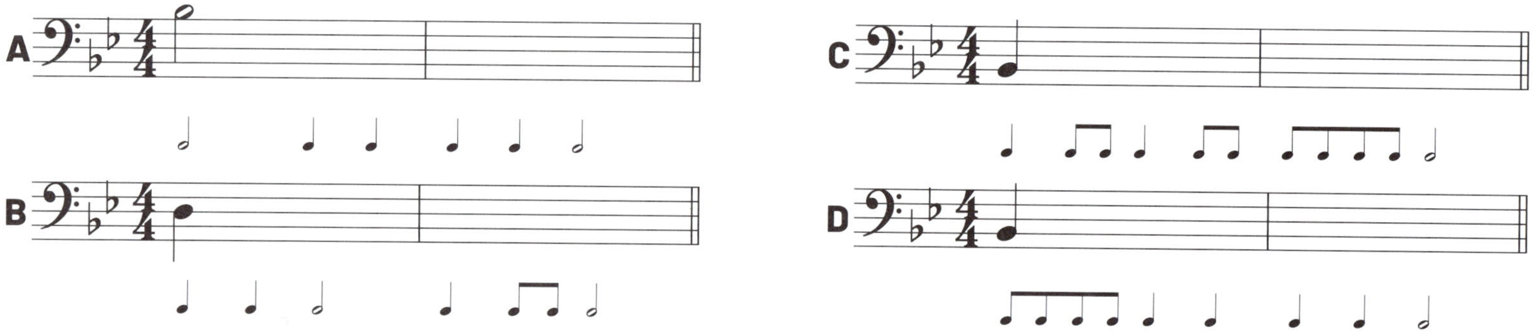

A

B

C

D

4. YOU NAME IT: ______________________________

Pick phrase A, B, C, or D from above, and write it as the "Question" for phrases 1 and 3 below. Then write 2 different "Answers" for phrases 2 and 4.

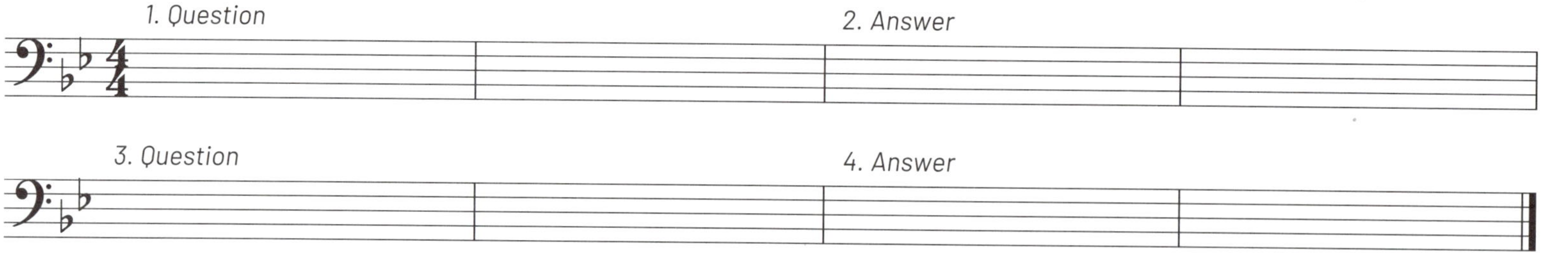

1. Question *2. Answer*

3. Question *4. Answer*

THEORY

Improvisation

Improvisation is the art of freely creating your own melody *as you play*. Use these notes to play your own melody (Line A), to go with the accompaniment (Line B).

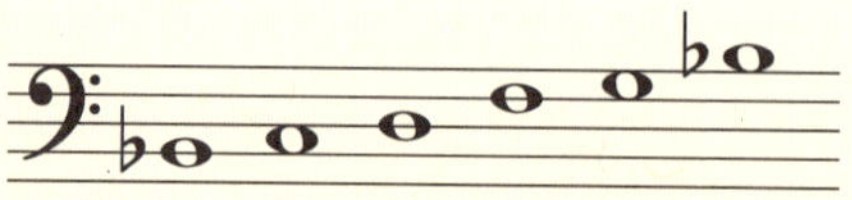

5. INSTANT MELODY

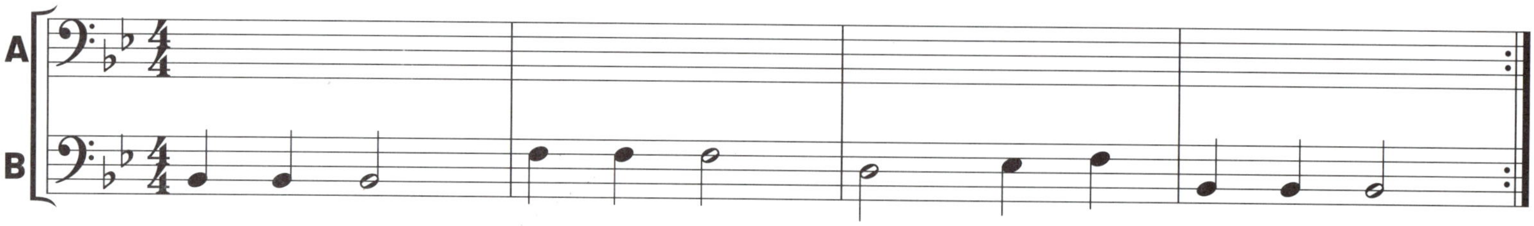

A

B

You can mark your progress through the book on this page.
Fill in the stars as instructed by your band director.

1. Page 2-3, The Basics
2. Page 5, EE Quiz, No. 13
3. Page 6, EE Quiz, No. 19
4. Page 7, EE Quiz, No. 26
5. Page 8, EE Quiz, No. 32
6. Page 10, EE Quiz, No. 45
7. Page 12-13, Performance Spotlight
8. Page 14, EE Quiz, No. 65
9. Page 15, Essential Creativity, No. 72
10. Page 17, EE Quiz, No. 84
11. Page 17, Essential Creativity, No. 85
12. Page 19, EE Quiz, No. 98
13. Page 20, Essential Creativity, No. 104
14. Page 21, No. 109
15. Page 22, EE Quiz, No. 117
16. Page 23, Performance Spotlight
17. Page 24, EE Quiz, No. 125
18. Page 26, Essential Creativity, No. 137
19. Page 28, No. 149
20. Page 28, EE Quiz, No. 151
21. Page 29, Performance Spotlight
22. Page 31, EE Quiz, No. 164
23. Page 32, EE Quiz, No. 168
24. Page 33, No. 174
25. Page 35, EE Quiz, No. 181
26. Page 36, Performance Spotlight
27. Page 37, Performance Spotlight
28. Page 38, Performance Spotlight

MUSIC — AN ESSENTIAL ELEMENT OF LIFE

FINGERING CHART

ELECTRIC BASS

Instrument Care Reminders

- Be sure your amplifier is turned off before plugging-in or unplugging the audio cable connecting it to your instrument.
- When unplugging a cable, hold it by the plug (not by the wire).
- After playing, wipe off the instrument and strings with a clean soft cloth. Return the instrument to its case.
- Close all the latches on your case when the instrument is inside.
- Keep all 4 strings in tune (at normal tension) to prevent warping of the neck.
- Your case is designed to hold only specific objects. If you force anything else into the case, it may damage your instrument.

strings

4th 3rd 2nd 1st

frets

1st
2nd
3rd
4th
5th

Fingerboard diagrams show where to play the notes. Circles are drawn on the diagram to indicate the fingers to be used to play the notes.

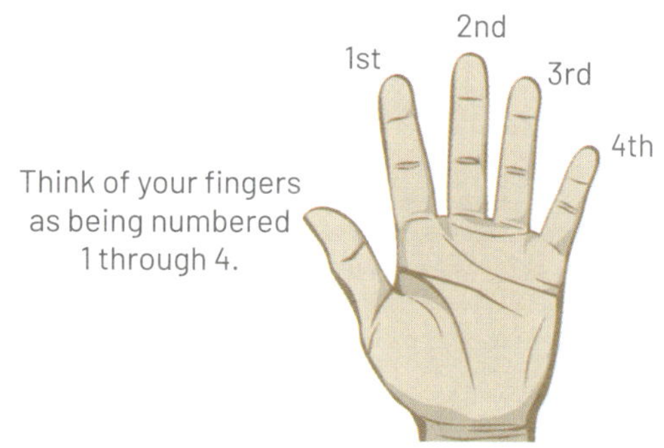

Think of your fingers as being numbered 1 through 4.

Instruments and photos courtesy of Yamaha.

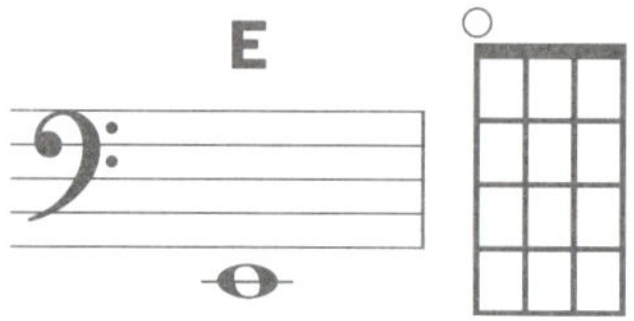

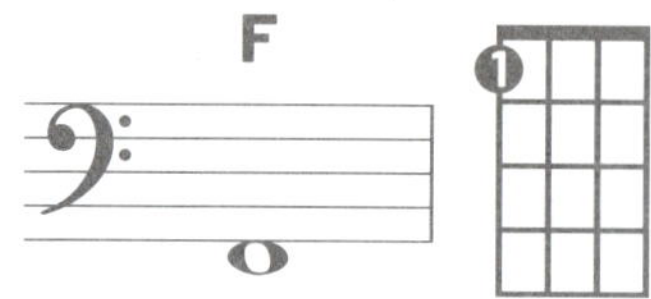

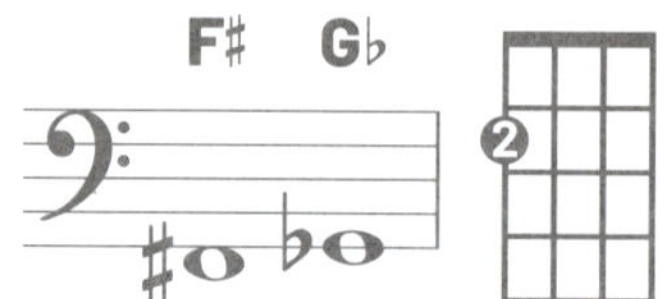

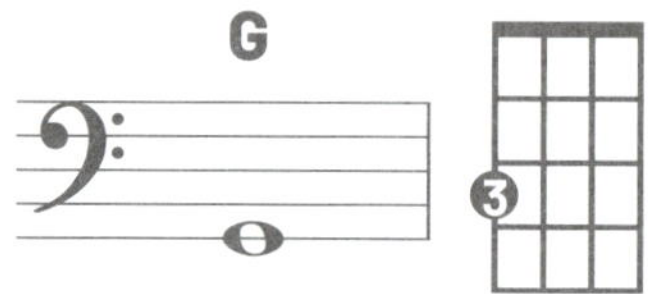

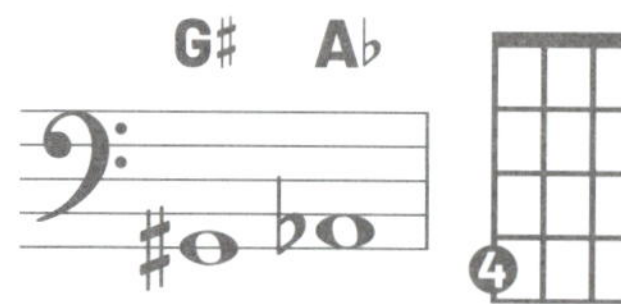

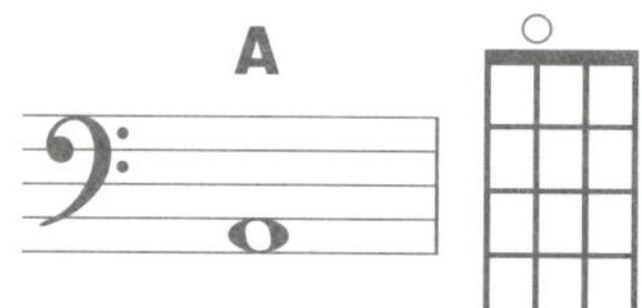

FINGERING CHART

ELECTRIC BASS

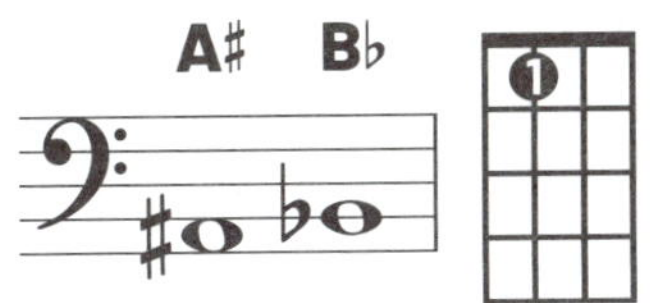

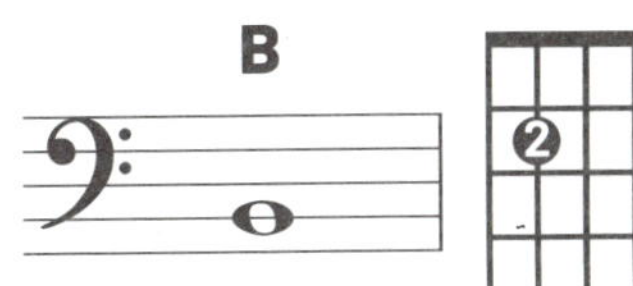

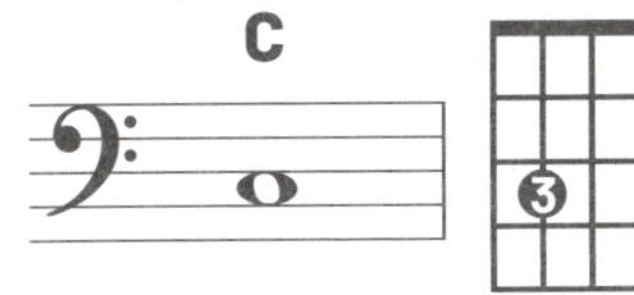

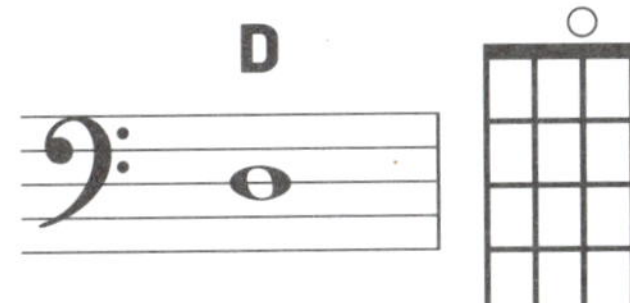

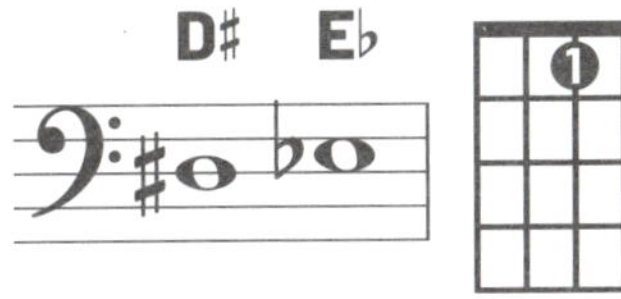

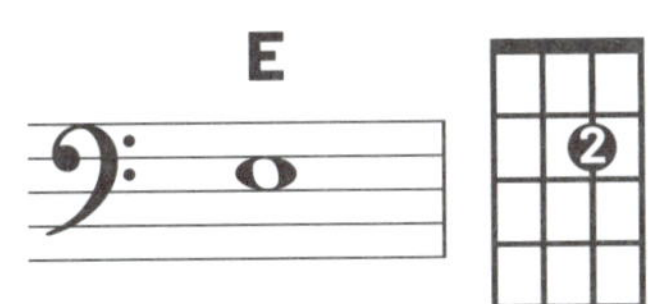

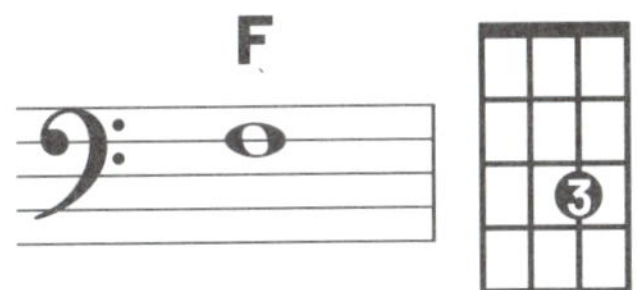

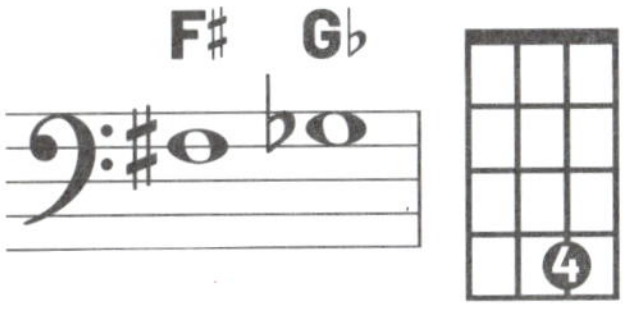

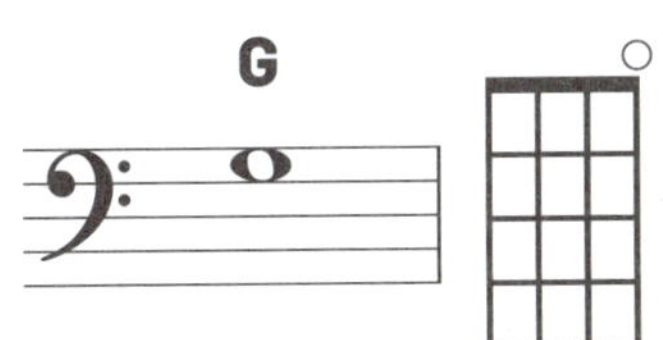

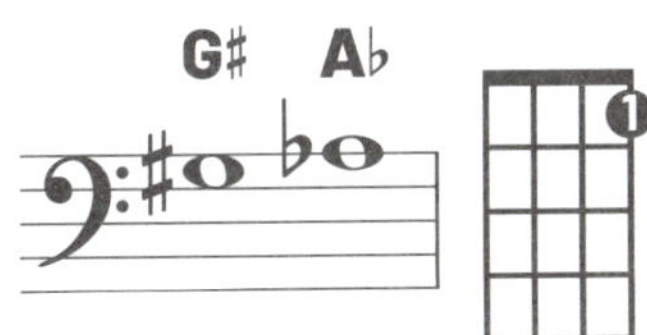

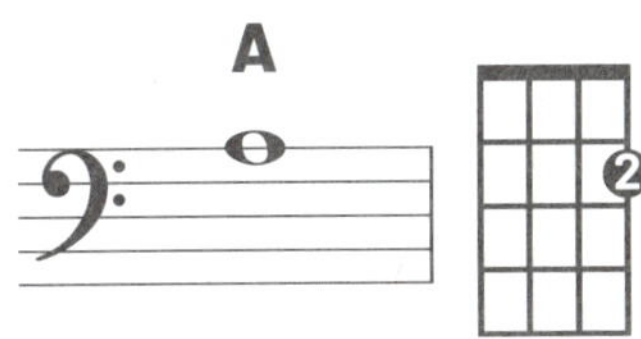

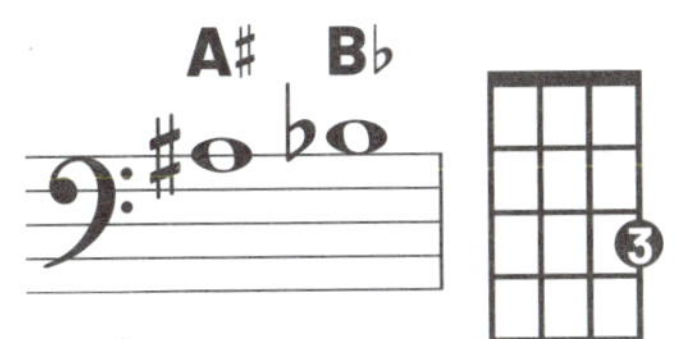

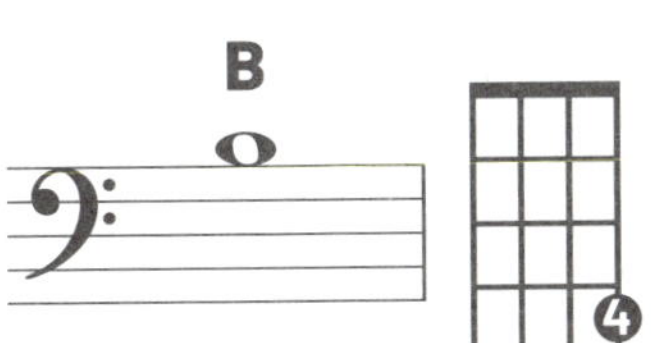

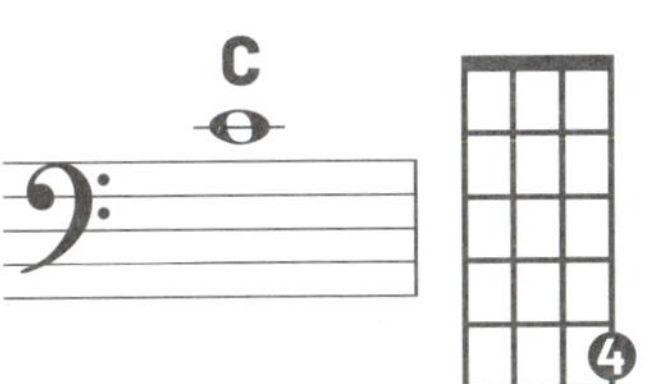

Reference Index

Definitions (pg.)

Composers

World Music